Let's Read! Storytime Crafts

Literacy Activities for Little Learners

Kathryn Totten

REMOVED FROM COLLECTION

UpstartBooks

Fort Atkinson, Wisconsin

WEST ISLIP PUBLIC LIBRARY
3 HIGBIE LANE
WEST ISLIP NEW YORK 11795

D1472440

Published by **UpstartBooks/Edupress**
W5527 Highway 106
P.O. Box 800
Fort Atkinson, Wisconsin 53538-0800

© Kathryn Totten, 2006
Cover design: Debra Neu

The paper used in this publication meets the minimum requirements of American National Standard for Information Sciences — Permanence of Paper for Printed Library Materials. ANSI/ NISO Z39.48-1992.

All rights reserved. Printed in the United States of America.
The purchase of this book entitles the individual librarian or teacher to reproduce copies for use in the library or classroom. The reproduction of any part for an entire school system or for commercial use is strictly prohibited. No form of this work may be reproduced, transmitted, or recorded without written permission from the publisher.

Contents

Introduction

The traditional library storytime has included reading books, storytelling, doing action rhymes, and singing songs. Storytime has been the first literary experience for countless children, and it provides learning experiences and opportunities beyond the printed word. Recent education theories support the role of storytime in emergent literacy. New best practices reflecting these theories are changing the traditional storytime in small but significant ways.

Multiple Intelligences

In 1983, Howard Gardner published *Frames of Mind: The Theory of Multiple Intelligences.* This work challenged former theories that human intelligence was hereditary and could be measured with IQ. Gardner believes that a multitude of intelligences exist. They are independent of each other, yet they are interrelated. At any one time, a child may be at different stages in these intelligences. They are often used at the same time and complement each other as children develop skills.

Gardner defined an intelligence as the capacity to solve problems in one or more cultural settings. The intelligences provide a new definition of human nature, cognitively speaking (Gardner, 1983). The intelligences he identified include: Linguistic, Logical-Mathematical, Musical, Visual, Bodily-Kinesthetic, Spatial, Interpersonal, Intrapersonal, and Naturalist. Each person has individual strengths, and will favor one or more of the intelligences.

What Constitutes an Emergent Literacy Storytime?

What is different about emergent literacy storytime? It is not so much a change in what we do, but in why we do it. The storytime presenter can adopt this motto—do nothing new, but do everything with a literacy purpose. Because each child has individual strengths, and will favor one or more of the intelligences. The storyteller should offer a variety of experiences at storytime. This helps each child discover his or her strengths, as well as develop the other intelligences.

Reading aloud is a key element of the traditional storytime. With a literacy focus, the read aloud experience becomes richer. In an emergent literacy storytime, the storyteller takes the time to show the cover of the book and state the title of the story before reading it. She teaches the child how to take care of a book and how to carefully turn the pages. The storyteller informs parents about how storytime fun supports their child's developing literacy. A Literacy Moment is directed at parents with each storytime. Occasionally, the storyteller points to the words on the page as she reads aloud. She indicates with her eyes and hands that reading goes from left to right. The storyteller includes letter recognition elements in the story extension activities. She selects books with rich language, to introduce new vocabulary words. All of these practices will strengthen Linguistic Intelligence.

Benefits of Storytelling for Literacy

Storytelling, a regular feature of traditional storytimes, is developing a stronger role in early literacy development. Storytelling enhances comprehension skills. It strengthens the capacity to create mental imagery. It introduces plot, setting, theme, and character. It gives children a framework for understanding written story texts, leading them from oral comprehension of language to reading comprehension.

Storytelling is a bonding experience between the storyteller and the listeners. The storyteller is offering a gift, her individual interpretation of a story! Listeners instinctively know this. The experience is fun, which is an important element for learning.

Hearing a story told by a skilled storyteller who uses inflection, gestures, and facial expressions gives listeners a role model for excellent communication. The use of correct grammar helps the listener develop an ear for the language. The use of pacing gives the listener time to visualize the story. The creative use of the voice gives the listener clues to the nature and appearance of the characters in the story. The skilled storyteller brings life to the story and greatly enhances the listening experience.

Cultural Literacy: Folktales and Nursery Rhymes

Including traditional rhymes and folktales helps ensure that the children in the storytime are building a repertoire of shared cultural building blocks for literature that they will encounter in the future. A child cannot understand a fractured fairy tale unless he or she is intimately acquainted with the original version. With a background in oral tradition, the child learns to communicate and to understand oral language. New vocabulary is introduced in the context of a story.

Cultural values, which have been developed through centuries, are communicated through traditional rhymes and folktales. Many of the parents in preschool storytimes are unfamiliar with traditional rhymes and folktales. Including the traditional stories fills in the gaps of their incomplete literary experiences, and gives them great stories to share at bedtime. Children should not grow up unaware of basic stories such as "Goldilocks and the Three Bears," "The Little Red Hen," and "The Three Little Pigs." Children should be able to recite many Mother Goose rhymes and other traditional rhymes.

The Whole Child Approach to Storytime Presentations

The well-prepared storytime benefits the whole child. At each storytime, several of the multiple intelligences are touched upon, and all of the intelligences are included over a period of several sessions. Although storytelling and the repetition of rhymes are literary experiences, they also strengthen other intelligences. The child's Interpersonal Intelligence is addressed with stories that illustrate cause and effect, consequences for actions, rewards for unselfishness, and good winning over bad. When the child begins to identify with the protagonist of the story, Intrapersonal Intelligence is developed. The repetition that is part of the structure of many folktales and nursery rhymes strengthens Logical-Mathematical Intelligence.

Including shape recognition in storytimes strengthens Spatial Intelligence. Teaching a child to recognize and name natural objects such as animals, flowers, dinosaurs, and fruits strengthens Naturalist Intelligence. Teaching a child to imitate rhythms with clapping games, and to match pitches through singing, strengthens Musical Intelligence. Action rhymes strengthen Bodily-Kinesthetic Intelligence. Art activities address Bodily-Kinesthetic Intelligence as well as Spatial Intelligence and Intrapersonal Intelligence.

The Role of Parents in Storytime

One of the most important elements of the early literacy storytime is the involvement of parents. They experience activities along with their children that are playful and enjoyable. They discover that these activities also help their child learn important skills. Parents can extend the storytime experience at home by singing, telling stories, reciting rhymes, and reading aloud with their child. When parents are given handouts they have the tools they need to continue storytime at home. Handouts may include recipes, art activities, and patterns for retelling stories and rhymes learned at storytime. It is a good practice to display many books at storytime in addition to the ones that were read. This encourages parents to check them out for reading at home. Parents who value literacy and model it at home are the best teachers for their children.

Storytime Themes

Bedtime

Before Sharing Books

Display a small blanket, a teddy bear, a pair of slippers, a pair of pajamas, a washcloth, a toothbrush, and a hairbrush. Using a puppet or doll, show how each of these items helps one get ready for bed at night.

Literacy Tip for Parents

After reading a book to your child, sometimes it is fun to recap the story. This helps your child learn sequencing.

Rhymes, Songs, and Fingerplays

Rhyme

"B" Rhyme for Bedtime
Letter Recognition

I like my **b**lue **b**lanket when I go to **b**ed.
It's the **b**est **b**lanket of all.
With **b**lue **b**lanket **b**eside me,
I'm **b**ound to **b**e **b**rave,
And I won't have **b**ad dreams, at all!

(Repeat the rhyme, and ask the children to raise their hands each time they hear a word that begins with the "B" sound.)

Song

"Goodnight Song"
Tune: "White Choral Bells"
Musical-Rhythmic Intelligence

Goodnight to you.
Sweet dreams as you sleep.

May the stars watch over you and safely keep.
Goodnight to me,
Here in my little bed.
May the moon shine softly on my little head.

Rhymes

Bounce Rhymes for Infant Storytime

I see the moon, and the moon sees me.
God bless the moon, and God bless me.

Sally go round the sun.
Sally go round the moon.
Sally go round the chimney pots
On a Sunday afternoon.

Nursery Rhyme for Cultural Awareness

Wee Willie Winkie runs through the town
Upstairs and downstairs, in his nightgown.
Rapping at the window, crying through the lock,
Are the children all in bed?
For now it's eight o'clock.

Books to Share

Bogan, Paulette. *Goodnight Lulu.* Bloomsbury Publishing, 2003. When her mother tucks her in for the night, Lulu the chicken worries about what would happen if a bear or a tiger or an alligator should come in during the night.

Dillon, Jana. *Upsie Downsie, Are You Asleep?* Pelican Publishing, 2002. Upsie Downsie convinces his mother he is having trouble falling asleep. She gets expert help from Miz Crumbsie, Mr. Humsie, Mayor Gumsie, and more. A wonderful story for phonemic awareness.

Gliori, Debi. *Polar Bolero.* Harcourt, 2001. When it is too hot to sleep, a polar bear goes outside and enjoys a nighttime dance before going to sleep. Gentle rhyme and imaginative illustrations make this a storytime favorite.

Jennings, Sharon. *No Monsters Here.* Fitzhenry & Whiteside, 2004. A brave little boy looks in the closet and behind the curtains to assure his father that there is nothing to fear at bedtime.

Wilson, Gina. *Grandma's Bears.* Candlewick Press, 2004. When Nat stays overnight with Grandma, he meets the bears that live with her. Grandma promises that the bears will like him, if he likes them. Nat and the bears help each other settle down for the night.

The Elves and the Shoemaker

Once upon a time there lived a poor shoemaker. He did the best work he could, but he was getting old and could not see well any more. The shoes he made were plain and simple and he sold just enough of them to get along without starving.

One night he went to bed without finishing the shoes he had begun. In the morning he found the job done. The stitches were so tiny and even! The shoes were buffed until they shone! He sold those shoes for a good price. During the day he set out all of the tools and material necessary to make another pair of shoes.

"Tomorrow morning, when the sun is shining and I can see well enough, I will begin working on them," he thought. But the next morning, instead of the leather he had left the night before, the shoemaker was very surprised to find a beautiful pair of brand-new shoes. Later on in the day, the customer came by the shop to see how his new shoes were coming along. When he found a nice pair of shoes ready, he was very happy and paid the shoemaker twice the price they had agreed upon.

The shoemaker was very confused and wondered what had happened. That night, he left out some more leather and the next morning he found another shiny and perfect pair of new shoes. These shoes were sold at an even higher price. Each night the shoemaker left out leather and tools and every morning, he found a new pair of shoes. Soon, the shoemaker was able to save a good sum of money. He bought his wife a fine coat, because it was wintertime and she did not have one.

"Thank you," she said. "But how can you afford to buy this for me?" The shoemaker explained that someone was helping him in the night, making fine shoes that sold for a good price. "Let's stay awake and watch tonight. We will hide and find out what is happening."

And so the shoemaker and his wife hid and, around midnight, they saw two elves sneak into the shoemaker's shop. The elves made a new pair of shoes in a flash. They wore only thin tunics without coats. Their feet were bare. They shivered while they worked.

"Poor fellows! They must be very cold," the shoemaker's wife whispered to her husband. "Tomorrow I will make them two heavy wool jackets."

"I will make them each a pair of boots, when the sun is bright enough for me to see my work," said the shoemaker. They completed their work the next day, and rested so they could stay awake and watch that night.

The following night, next to the leather, the two elves found two red wool jackets and two pairs of brown leather boots. They put on the jackets and boots and danced about the shop. Then they set to work, making the most beautiful pair of shoes the shoemaker had ever seen. When they were finished, they danced away on a moonbeam.

The fine pair of shoes sold for a great price. The shoemaker and his wife retired. The shoe shop was closed for good. They lived comfortably all their days, but they never saw the elves again.

Adapted from a story by Jacob Grimm.

Bedtime Bear

Directions

Copy the pattern and cut it out. Have the children dress the bear in his pajamas by pasting them on using a glue stick. They may also want to color the pajamas with crayons.

 This craft takes 5 minutes to complete.

Birthdays

Before Sharing Books

Dress a puppet in a party hat and a nice party outfit. Have the children sing "Happy Birthday" to the puppet. Dedicate today's storytime to him to celebrate his birthday.

Literacy Tip for Parents

Toddlers understand more words than they are able to say, so be sure to talk to them all day long about what you are doing together.

Rhymes, Songs, and Fingerplays

Rhyme

My Birthday Party
Letter Recognition

I'm having a party.
It's my birthday tonight.
I know we'll have fun.
Who shall I invite?

I will invite "B,"
To bring some balloons.
I will invite "C,"
To bring cupcakes, too.
I will invite "P,"
To bring presents to share.
I will invite "H,"
To bring hats to wear.

(Use the patterns on page 14 to create flannel board figures to use with this rhyme.)

Song

"It's My Happy Day" *Tune: "Mary Had a Little Lamb"*
Musical-Rhythmic Intelligence

It's my happy day today,
Sing and play, sing and play!
It's my birthday! Celebrate.
Let's eat some cake today.

Action Rhymes

I Am Bigger
Bodily-Kinesthetic Intelligence
From my head to my middle,
(Touch head, touch waist.)
I have grown, grown, grown.
(Hands over head.)
From my middle to my toes,
(Touch waist, touch toes.)
I have grown.
(Hands over head.)
From my head to my middle,
(Touch head, touch waist.)
From my middle to my toes.
(Touch waist, touch toes.)
I am bigger. *(Hands over head.)*
I have grown, grown, grown.

Bounce Rhymes for Infant Storytime

Diddle diddle dumpling,
My son John,
Went to bed with his stockings on.
One shoe off and one shoe on,
Diddle diddle dumpling,
My son John.

Dickory, dickory, dare,
The pig flew up in the air,
The man in brown
Soon brought him down,
Dickory, dickory, dare.

Rhyme

Nursery Rhyme for Cultural Awareness
There was a maid on Scrabble Hill,
And, if not dead, she lives there still.
She grew so tall, she reached the sky,
And on the moon hung clothes to dry.

Books to Share

Fernandes, Eugenie. *Big Week for Little Mouse.* Kids Can Press, 2004. Little Mouse spends all week preparing for her birthday party.

Parr, Todd. *Otto Has a Birthday.* Little, Brown and Company, 2004. When Otto the dog decides to bake a cake for his birthday party, he includes shoes, bones, and a cootie bug in the cake batter! When his friends come for the party, Otto opens the oven door and his cake does not look right!

Riddell, Chris. *Platypus and the Birthday Party.* Harcourt, 2003. Platypus plans a birthday party for Bruce, his favorite stuffed animal. He has party hats, decorations, and games ready. But something is missing.

Wallace, John. *Tiny Rabbit Goes to a Birthday Party.* Holiday House, 2000. Tiny Rabbit is invited to his first birthday party. He tries on several costumes before deciding what to wear. He tries to think of the perfect present. When he arrives at the party, he is shy, until someone invites him to play.

Wormell, Mary. *Hilda Hen's Happy Birthday.* Harcourt, 1995. Hilda Hen eats oats, apples, and cookies she finds around the farmyard, thinking they are birthday gifts left by her friends. The other hens save the day.

The Three Wishes

Once upon a time, a poor woodsman lived in a great forest. Every day he kissed his good wife and then went out into the woods to cut down trees. He found a huge old oak tree, which he was sure would be worth plenty when properly cut. So the woodsman raised his ax high! But before he could strike one blow, he heard a sad, sad sound.

"Please don't cut this tree!" a tiny voice cried.

The woodsman looked around, but he could not see anyone. He raised his ax again, but the voice called once more, "Please don't cut this tree!"

The woodsman was a kind man. He looked high and low, but did not see anyone. He called out, speaking to whomever it might be, "I will not cut the tree. Don't worry. I will spare this tree today because today is my birthday."

Suddenly a tiny man appeared, standing by the oak tree. "You have done well, sir," said the little man. "Now I will do something for you! I will grant to you and your good wife the next three wishes you wish for. Happy birthday, sir." Then the little man disappeared, leaving only his tiny hat behind.

The woodsman did no more work that day! He picked up the little hat and ran all the way home. He sat by the fire, tired from running and not just a little bit hungry. He looked about the kitchen for something to eat, but nothing was cooking. It was a long time until supper.

"Have you anything to eat?" he asked his wife.

"Not for a couple of hours yet," she answered.

"But I am hungry now!" groaned the woodsman. "I wish I had a big fat sausage to eat." No sooner had he said it, when there on the table was the biggest sausage a man could wish for. The woodsman smiled, and reached for it! What a nice birthday meal it would make. But his wife slapped his hand.

"What's all this?" she asked. The woodsman told her then about the old oak tree, the little man, and the three wishes. He showed her the little hat, to prove the story was true.

"Fool!" she shouted, shaking her finger at him. "You have spent one good wish on a sausage! I wish that sausage was on the end of your nose!" Quick as a wink, the sausage flew off the table and attached to the end of the woodsman's nose.

He gave a pull, but it stuck. She gave a pull, but it stuck. They both pulled the sausage until his nose was red and sore, but the sausage was stuck for good.

"What will I do now?" the woodsman said with a sigh. "Two wishes are gone, and I am still hungry. What a miserable birthday this has turned out to be."

"I think it makes you look handsome," said the woodsman's wife, smiling at him. "Leave it there, and wish for gold or jewels," she suggested.

"No," said the woodsman. "A birthday meal is what I wanted, and that is still what I want. I wish the sausage was on the table, hot and ready to eat."

Quick as a wink, it was. So, although the woodsman and his wife did not have gold or jewels, they had a fine supper, and a tiny hat to remind them of their three wishes.

This folktale is from England. Adapted from a story collected by Joseph Jacobs.

My Birthday Party

B is for Birthday and Balloons

Directions
Copy the coloring sheet for each child. Help them recognize the letter "B" for "birthday" and "balloons." Have them color the picture with crayons or markers.

 This craft takes 5 minutes to complete.

Bubbles

Before Sharing Books

Set out some bath supplies, such as a soft face cloth, shampoo, a bath toy, a bar of soap, a baby bathtub, etc. You may also want to bring a jar of bubble liquid so you can blow a few bubbles for the children.

Literacy Tip for Parents

Make bath time a learning experience. Draw letters with soap crayons. Count fingers and toes. Sing or recite rhymes while bathing.

Rhymes, Songs, and Fingerplays

Rhyme

Five Little Bubbles
Logical-Mathematical Intelligence

Five little bubbles, I wish there were more!
I popped one and then there were four.
Four little bubbles, fragile as can be.
I popped one and then there were three.
Three little bubbles shiny and blue.
I popped one and then there were two.
Two little bubbles, having so much fun!
I popped one and then there was one.
One little bubble, floating all alone.
I popped it, too, and then there were none.

(Encourage the children to clap in the air, pretending to pop each bubble as you recite the rhyme.)

Rhymes

Bath Shapes
Spatial Intelligence

Rectangle soap, and square washcloth,
Lots of round bubbles, pop, pop, pop!

Bounce Rhymes for Infant Storytime

Rub a dub dub,
Three men in a tub,
And who do you think they be?
The butcher, the baker, the candlestick maker,
Turn them out, knaves all three.

Bell horses, bell horses,
What time of day?
One o'clock, two o'clock,
Time to away.

Nursery Rhymes for Cultural Awareness

There was a little girl who had a little curl
Right in the middle of her forehead.
When she was good she was very, very good,
And when she was bad, she was horrid.

Swan swam over the sea.
Swim, swan, swim!
Swan swam back again.
Well swum, swan.

Books to Share

Arnold, Tedd. *Huggly Takes a Bath.* Scholastic, 1999. Huggly, the monster under the bed, wants a bath! He washes his toes with toothbrushes and uses lots of liquid soap to make bubbles. When he's covered in fluffy white bubbles, a sleepy child mistakes him for a ghost.

Johnson, Jane. *Little Bunny's Bathtime.* Tiger Tales, 2004. Little bunny doesn't want a bath with his siblings, but he does want his mother's attention.

Krosoczka, Jarrett. *Bubble Bath Pirates.* Viking, 2003. Young pirates walk the plank into the frothy tub, shouting, "Yo ho, yo ho, it's off to the bath we go."

Puttock, Simon. *Squeaky Clean.* Little, Brown and Company, 2002. The three little pigs hate baths, but Mrs. Pig entices them to the tub with bubbles, rubber ducks, and splooshes. They have so much fun, they want to get dirty again and take another bath.

Soap! Soap! Soap!

One day a woman was getting ready to do her laundry. She built a fire. She put her big kettle over it, and filled it with water. Then she discovered she was out of soap. So she called her little boy. "Here is some money. Go to the store and buy some soap."

"I will," he said.

"Don't forget. Just keep saying 'soap, soap' until you get to the store."

So the boy walked along. He kept saying "Soap ... soap ... soap!"

It had rained the day before and the dirt road was pretty muddy. The boy stepped into a muddy pothole. He stumbled and almost slipped. But when he caught his balance, he'd forgotten what he was supposed to get. He kept walking through the muddy spot, saying, "I lost it, I lost it." Soon the boy had made a big, slick, muddy patch in the road.

A man came walking up the road. He slipped in the muddy patch the boy's pacing had made and exclaimed, "This spot is slicker than soap!" When the boy heard this, he grinned and said, "Soap! ... Soap! ... Soap!" He jumped up and down, pleased that he remembered what he was supposed to buy. But the man thought the boy was teasing him. "Don't tease me, son. Say you are sorry."

"Sorry," said the boy. And he ran down the road saying, "Sorry ... sorry ... sorry." He couldn't remember what he was going to the store for.

He ran around a corner and bumped right into an old lady. She was carrying a basket full of milk and eggs. The basket flew into the ditch. The eggs broke and the milk spilled. "Sorry," said the boy crying.

"Child, you just busted my eggs and spilled my milk."

"Sorry," said the boy.

"I know you are sorry, son. Please get me my basket out of the ditch." The boy fetched her basket and got broken egg and milky mud all over himself. As he climbed out of the ditch with the lady's basket, he was still crying, "Sorry."

"That's all right, child, I know you are sorry," said the woman. "There's no use crying over spilt milk."

The boy headed on down the road and he still couldn't remember what he was going to get. He just kept saying "Spilt milk ... spilt milk."

Then he came upon the milkman whose wagon had gotten stuck in the ditch. The milkman was trying to push it out. He heard the boy repeating. "Spilt milk ... spilt milk."

"It isn't spilt yet, boy. Can't you see? I need help."

So the boy got in the muddy ditch behind the wagon and after a lot of shoving and shouting at the mule, and a couple of falls flat on his face, the wagon was freed. The man thanked him and drove his wagon off.

When the boy reached town, he still couldn't remember what he had been sent to get. He just kept crying and saying, "Can't you see? Can't you see?" Just in front of the store he met an old man with a white cane. The old man said. "I can't see, but I sure can smell. You sure do stink! You need a bath, I think!"

"Need a bath, I think! Need a bath, I think!" repeated the boy as he entered the store.

The woman behind the counter looked him over. He was dirty from top to bottom. He had mud, egg shells, and milk all over himself. His face was black and streaked from crying and rubbing his eyes with dirty hands.

"You sure do need a bath, boy. And you'd better use lots of soap," she said.

"Soap! SOAP!" said the boy. "That's what I need, soap!" He bought the soap and went straight home.

When he got home, his mother took a long look at him. "You sure do stink! You need a bath, I think!" she said.

She grabbed the soap in one hand and his hand in the other. She put him in the tub, clothes and all. She poured in some warm water. She soaped him up and scrubbed him down three times, until all the mud and dirt and eggs and milk was gone and he was clean and smelling sweet. Then she took two clothespins and hung him on the clothesline, clothes and all, to dry until she had finished the rest of her laundry.

Adapted from a folktale in Grandfather Tales *by Richard Chase.*

Bubbles for Rubber Ducky

Directions

Copy the picture of the rubber ducky for each child. Show the children how to draw a circle shape on a white board or a piece of paper. Help them draw circles in the air with their finger. Have them draw some circular bubbles around the rubber ducky with a crayon.

 This craft takes 10 minutes to complete, including the circle practice and art activity.

Cars

Before Sharing Books

Display a variety of toy cars. Lead the children in an imagination exercise: "We are going on a pretend car trip for storytime. Everyone has to climb into their car seat and fasten the seat belt. We have to shut the doors and roll up the windows. We turn on the car with a key, can you hear it? Vroom, vroom! Off we go!"

Literacy Tip for Parents

While driving around on errands, point out colors on signs and other surroundings. "The stop sign is red. The car next to us is blue. The trees are green."

Rhymes, Songs, and Fingerplays

Song

"The Windows on the Car"
Tune: "The Wheels on the Bus"
Musical Intelligence

The windows in the car go up and down,
Up and down, up and down.
The windows in the car go up and down,
All through the town.

Additional verses:
The seat belts in the car go click, click, click.
The engine in the car goes vroom,
   vroom, vroom.
The children in the car say, "Here we go."
The driver in the car turns left and right.

Rhyme

Slug Bug Game

I am looking for a slug bug.
I see one!
Looking for slug bugs is lots of fun.
What color is the slug bug?
Can you say?
I see a blue slug bug today.

*(You may want to create several colors of "Slug Bugs" for the flannel board to use with this rhyme. You may also include cars of other shapes, helping the children recognize the shape of a Volkswagon Beetle. Talk about the game of "Slug Bug." The rules: while driving in your car, when you see a Volkswagon Beetle, you tap someone next to you **lightly** on the arm and say "Slug Bug green" or any other color. Try to find the most Slug Bugs.)*

Song

"Did You Ever Find The Car Keys?" *Tune: "Did You Ever See a Lassie?"*
Musical Intelligence

Did you ever find the car keys,
The car keys, the car keys.
Did you ever find the car keys,
Under the couch?
We looked this way and that way,
And this way and that way.
Then we found the car keys,
Under the couch!

Additional verses: Under the dog, Inside the sink, Next to the phone, Inside the fridge, etc.
(Try making up more verses with the children, the sillier the better.)

Rhymes

Bounce Rhymes for Infant Storytime

Smiling girls, rosy boys,
Come and buy my little toys—
Monkeys made of gingerbread,
And sugar horses painted red.

Pussycat, pussycat, where have you been?
I've been to London to visit the queen.
Pussycat, pussycat, what did you do there?
I frightened a little mouse under her chair.

Nursery Rhyme for Cultural Awareness

From Wibbleton to Wobbleton is fifteen miles.
From Wobbleton to Wibbleton is fifteen miles.
From Wibbleton to Wobbleton,
From Wobbleton to Wibbleton,
From Wibbleton to Wobbleton is fifteen miles.

Books to Share

Hall, Kirsten. *Zoom, Zoom, Zoom.* Scholastic Library Publishing, 2004. While playing with his new toy car, a boy imagines that he is driving all over town.

Howland, Naomi. *ABCDrive! A Car Trip Alphabet.* Houghton Mifflin, 1994. A family on a car trip sees things for every letter of the alphabet, including an ambulance, a bus, and a cement mixer.

Root, Phyllis. *Rattletrap Car.* Candlewick Press, 2001. As Poppa and the children drive to the lake in their rattletrap car, many problems arise, but they come up with a funny, creative solution for each one.

Steen, Sandra. *Car Wash.* Penguin, 2001. Dad tells the twins, "Lunchtime!," and they pile into the car and head down the road. But a huge puddle splatters the car with mud, so they head for the car wash!

Wagner, Jenny. *Motor Bill and the Lovely Caroline.* Ticknor & Fields, 1995. Everyone likes Bill, but no one believes in his car except Caroline, who goes on a picnic with him.

The Cock, the Cat, and the Mouse

Once upon a time a little mouse decided to go on a car trip to see the world. He packed some bread and cheese in a little basket to eat on the way. He locked the door of his house, climbed into his little car, and set off for his adventure.

He drove past a yellow house, a blue house, and a green house. They were the last three houses on his street. Soon he was in the countryside, where he had never been before. The little mouse drove past tall trees and rolling countryside. He saw many color-ful flowers and butterflies. He drove for a few hours, until he was tired out. He pulled off the road in front of a little cottage with a fence. It did not look like the houses on his street. After eating some of his bread and cheese, he thought he would see what sort of place this house in the country was.

The little mouse walked through the gate. There in the yard he saw two strange animals he had never seen before. One was large and furry. It had four legs. On its face were white whiskers. The creature was sleeping peacefully in the shade of a tree. "How wise and gentle this creature seems," thought the mouse.

The other strange animal had two legs. It had red, yellow, and green feathers stick-ing out all over. It had a mean face! It had a sharp, pointy yellow beak. It had cruel eyes that stared at the little mouse. The little mouse held out his hand and said, "How do you do?" But the creature just puffed out its chest and made a horrible noise!

"Cocka-doodle-doo!" the creature cried, and it strutted towards the mouse. The little mouse saw the big yellow beak hovering over him. "I must run!" he squeaked. He turned and ran away fast!

The little mouse saw a hole in the wall. He wiggled through the hole and saw three faces staring at him. They were mouse faces, of course, which made him feel much better. "Where did you come from?" one of them asked.

"I've come ..." gasped the little mouse breath-lessly, "... from far away! Where am I now?"

"This is our home. We're field mice. What happened?" And the little mouse told them about the animals he had met in the farm-yard—one harmless creature with pretty fur and whiskers, the other one, very mean and covered with feathers.

The three field mice laughed. "Calm down, friend," said one of the field mice. "You are safe now."

"Pull up a chair," said another field mouse. "I'll fix you a cup of tea."

"Good thing you got away!" said the third field mouse. "You were in more danger than you know. The strange animal that scared you is only a rooster. He acts mean, but he is harmless. The other strange animal, with the pretty fur and whiskers, is the cat! If he had seen you, you wouldn't be here to tell the tale. As you see, you can't always judge by appearances!"

Retold from a story collected by Joseph Jacobs.

Slug Bug on the Road

Directions

Copy the "Slug Bug" pattern on colored paper for each child and cut it out. For each child, draw a dotted line along the middle of a sheet of black construction paper, using a white crayon or white chalk. This will be the dividing line on the road. At storytime, have each child paste the car on the road with a glue stick.

 This craft takes 10 minutes to complete.

Colorful World

Before Sharing Books

Display a big bowl of fruits in many varieties. Pick up each one and ask the children to tell you what color it is. Name a child who is wearing that color. Continue with all of the items in the bowl.

Literacy Tip for Parents

While dressing your child, talk about colors and numbers. "Let's put on your red T-shirt. Here are your two white socks."

Rhymes, Songs, and Fingerplays

Action Rhyme

Colorful World
Bodily-Kinesthetic Intelligence

Blue sky. *(Arms over head.)*
White snow. *(Touch the ground.)*
Yellow sun. *(Arms over head.)*
Pink *(or brown)* toes. *(Touch toes.)*
Green plants all around. *(Turn in a circle.)*
Many-colored butterflies, all sit down. *(Flap your wings, then sit down.)*

Rhyme

Flower Garden
Naturalist Intelligence

Yellow tulips,
In a row.
Orange poppies,
Seem to glow.
Roses red,
Daisies white.
Purple Iris,
What a sight!
Flower garden,
You can grow,
Every color,
That I know.

(You may want to show pictures of these flowers, and help the children learn to identify them by shape and color.)

Song

"Did You Ever See A Blue Cat?"
Tune: "Did You Ever See A Lassie?"
Musical Intelligence

Did you ever see a blue cat,
A blue cat, a blue cat?
Did you ever see a blue cat,
In your front yard?
I never, no never,
No never, no never!
I never saw a blue cat,
In my front yard.

Repeat with: Green horse, red mouse, orange cow, etc. Use the patterns on page 28 to create magnet or flannel board figures to use with this song, if desired.

Action Rhymes

Big R and Little R
Bodily-Kinesthetic Intelligence and Letter Recognition

Big R and Little R,
Ran through the rain.
They ran through the puddles,
Splashed again and again.
They ran around the big tree.
They ran across the lawn.
They ran 'til they were tired.
Little R said with a yawn,
"I want to go home. I want a snack."
So Big R said,
"I'll race you back!"

(Coach the children to pat their hands on their lap each time they hear the word "ran.")

Bounce Rhymes for Infant Storytime

Hickey, pickety, my black hen.
She lays eggs for gentlemen.
Gentlemen come every day,
To see what my black hen doth lay.

Sing, sing,
What shall I sing?
The cat's run away,
With the pudding string.
Do, do,
What shall I do?
The cat's run away,
With the pudding, too!

Nursery Rhyme for Cultural Awareness

Little Boy Blue,
Come blow your horn.
The sheep's in the meadow.
The cow's in the corn.
Where is the boy who looks after the sheep?
He is under the haystack, fast asleep.
Will you wake him?
No, not I.
For if I do,
He is sure to cry.

Books to Share

Bruce, Lisa. *Patterns in the Park.* Raintree Publishers, 2004. Simple text shows patterns made of different shapes that can be found in a park.

Dodd, Emma. *Dog's Colorful Day.* Penguin, 2001. A colorful story about a sloppy dog who gets ten different colored spots on him through his day.

Grace, Will. *Caterpillar Dance.* Scholastic, 2004. Count backward from five to one as caterpillars turn into beautiful butterflies. The book has die-cut pages with reflective material and toy caterpillars.

Spanyol, Jessica. *Carlo Likes Colors.* Candlewick Press, 2003. Carlo the giraffe sees colors in a variety of places, including red in the street, brown in the woods, and orange at a café.

Spurr, Elizabeth. *Farm Life.* Holiday House, 2003. Rhymed descriptions of life on a farm introduce basic colors and the numbers from one to ten.

Little Red Riding Hood

Once upon a time at the edge of the woods there was a pretty little house. This house was the home of a pretty little girl. This girl was known to everyone as Little Red Riding Hood. Of course, that was because she always wore her red cloak with a hood.

One day, her mother sent her off, saying, "Grandma is under the weather. Seeing you would make her feel better. Take her this basket of good food, but be very careful. Keep to the path through the woods and don't ever stop. That way, you will come to no harm."

Little Red Riding Hood gave her mother a big hug and said, "Don't worry, Mother. I'll run all the way to Grandma's without stopping."

Little Red Riding Hood meant to keep to the path, just as her mother asked. But when she saw some lovely red strawberries, she just forgot. Laying her basket on the ground, Little Red Riding Hood bent over the strawberry plants. "They're nice and ripe, and so big! Yummy! Delicious!" She picked one, two, three, and many more.

Little Red Riding Hood did not see two wicked eyes that were spying on her from behind a tree. She heard a strange rustling in the woods. It made Little Red Riding Hood's heart thump and she remembered what her mother told her.

"I must find the path and run away from here!" She picked up her basket and ran. At last she reached the path again, but she jumped at the sound of a gruff voice that said, "Where are you going, little girl? You should not be all alone in the woods."

Little Red Riding Hood found herself staring at a wolf. Bravely she answered his question. "I'm taking Grandma some good food. She lives at the end of the path," said Little Riding Hood.

When he heard this, the wolf politely asked, "Does Grandma live by herself?"

"Oh, yes," replied Little Red Riding Hood, "and she never opens the door to strangers!"

"Goodbye. Perhaps we'll meet again," replied the wolf. Then he ran away thinking to himself, I'll gobble the grandmother first. She will be just a snack. When the girl arrives, she will be dessert!

When he arrived at the end of the path, the cottage came in sight. The wolf ran to the door and knocked. Knock! Knock!

"Who's there?" cried Grandma from her bed.

The crafty old wolf changed his voice. He made it sound like a little girl's voice. "It's me, Little Red Riding Hood. I've brought you some good food because you're ill."

"Come in," said Grandma. She believed the wolf's lies. Poor Grandma! For in one bound, the wolf leapt across the room and, in a single mouthful, swallowed the old lady. Soon after, Little Red Riding Hood tapped on the door.

"Grandma, can I come in?" she called.

The wolf had put on the old lady's extra nightgown and cap. He was tucked under a quilt in her bed. Trying to imitate Grandma's quavering little voice, he replied, "Come in!

"Grandma! What a deep voice you have," said Little Red Riding Hood.

"The better to greet you with, my dear," said the wolf.

Little Red Riding Hood came closer. "Grandma! Goodness, what big eyes you have."

"The better to see you with, my dear," said the wolf.

Little Red Riding Hood came closer. "Grandma! What big hands you have!" exclaimed Little Red Riding Hood, stepping close to the bed.

"The better to hug you with, my dear," said the wolf.

There was a little quiver of fear in her voice when Little Red Riding Hood said, "Grandma. What a big mouth you have."

"The better to eat you with, my dear!" growled the wolf. He jumped out of bed and swallowed her in one gulp! Then, with a fat full tummy, he fell fast asleep.

Just then, a hunter emerged from the woods. He decided to stop at the cottage and ask for a drink. The hunter had been following the tracks of a big wolf that had been stealing sheep and chickens from other homes in the woods. But the hunter had lost the wolf's tracks. The hunter could hear a strange whistling sound coming from inside the cottage. He peered through the window and saw the wolf dressed in a nightgown! He was snoring away in Grandma's bed.

He jumped back in surprise! "The wolf! He won't get away this time!"

Without making a sound, the hunter carefully loaded his gun and gently opened the window. He pointed the barrel straight at the wolf's head. The wolf woke up and saw the hunter. He was so frightened, he burped! Out popped Grandma and Little Red Riding Hood, safe and unharmed.

"You arrived just in time," said Grandma. Around and around the cottage, the hunter chased the wolf. At last he caught him and tied him up! "I'll be taking this wolf with me," said the hunter.

"Take him far away!" said Little Red Riding Hood.

"It's safe to go home now," the hunter told Little Red Riding Hood. "The big bad wolf is gone, and there is no danger on the path. The hunter and the wolf went away. Little Red Riding Hood hugged her grandmother. They were exhausted! They curled up together on the bed and fell asleep.

Much later, as dusk was falling, Little Red Riding Hood's mother arrived at Grandma's cottage. She was worried because her little girl had not come home. When she saw Little Red Riding Hood, safe and sound, she burst into tears of joy. The three of them spent the night together, eating the good food from the basket and warming their toes by the fire.

In the morning, Little Red Riding Hood and her mother set off towards their home at the edge of woods. As they walked quickly through the trees, the little girl told her mother: "We must always keep to the path and never stop. That way, we come to no harm!"

Adapted from a story collected by Jacob Grimm.

"Did You Ever See a Blue Cat" Patterns

Color Collage

Directions
Cut a variety of the above shapes from colored paper. Have the children create a picture by gluing the colored shapes on construction paper with a glue stick.

 This craft takes 5 minutes to complete.

Counting

Before Sharing Books

Be creative and bring a variety of items to display. Spend a few minutes counting things with the children—books you have on your table, figures on your flannel board, teddy bears, building blocks, fingers on one hand, etc. Congratulate them for counting so well.

Literacy Tip for Parents

If you frequently point out words in books and on signs that contain the letters of your child's name, he or she will soon find the letters everywhere on his or her own.

Rhymes, Songs, and Fingerplays

Action Rhyme

I Have Two Eyes
Bodily-Kinesthetic Intelligence

I have two eyes,
And ten little toes.
I have two hands,
But just one nose.
I have two ears,
Two legs that run,
And ten little fingers,
For tickle fun.

Song

"Ten Little Teddies"
Tune: "Ten Little Indians"
Musical Intelligence and Logical-Mathematical Intelligence

One little, two little, three little teddies.
Four little, five little, six little teddies.
Seven little, eight little, nine little teddies.
Ten little teddy bears!

(Use the pattern on page 10 to make ten flannel board teddy bears to use with this song.)

Rhymes

Bounce Rhymes for Infant Storytime

Wash the dishes,
Wipe the dishes,
Ring the bell for tea.
Three good wishes,
Three good kisses,
I will give to thee.
One, two, three, four,
Mary's at the cottage door.
Five, six, seven, eight,
Eating cherries off a plate.

Nursery Rhyme for Cultural Awareness

Sing a song of sixpence,
A pocket full of rye.
Four and twenty blackbirds,
Baked in a pie.
When the pie was opened,
The birds began to sing.
Wasn't that a dainty dish,
To set before the king?

Books to Share

Bajaj, Varsha. *How Many Kisses Do You Want Tonight?* Little, Brown and Company, 2004. When bedtime comes, the parents of a girl, a boy, and various animals ask their children how many kisses they want.

Bruce, Lisa. *Counting at a Birthday Party.* Raintree Publishers, 2004. Uses simple, rhyming text to count the items at a birthday party.

DiPucchio, Kelly. *Bed Hogs.* Hyperion, 2004. Hoping to get some sleep, Little Runt boots his hog family

out of bed one by one, but finds that he needs them back again.

Thompson, Lauren. *Little Quack's Hide and Seek.* Simon & Schuster, 2004. Little Quack and his siblings play hide and seek with Mama as she counts to ten.

Thong, Roseanne. *One Is a Drummer.* Chronicle Books, 2004. A young girl numbers her discoveries in the world around her, from one dragon boat to four mahjong players to ten bamboo stalks.

The Three Little Pigs

(Suggestion: Use this story with children age 4 and up)

There was an old mother pig with three little pigs. When the three little pigs were big enough, she sent them out to seek their fortune. "Good-bye, and be wise," she said as she kissed each one on his hairy little pig nose.

The first little pig walked along until he met a man with a bundle of straw. "Please give me that straw so I may build myself a house," said the little pig. The man gave him the straw, and the little pig built a house with it in one hour!

Just as the little pig was moving in, along came the big bad wolf. He knocked at the door, and said, "Little pig, little pig, let me come in."

The first little pig answered, "Not by the hair of my chinny chin chin."

"Then I'll huff and I'll puff and I'll blow your house in." So he huffed and he puffed and he blew his house in, and the first little pig ran down the road as fast as he could to find his brothers.

The second little pig met a man with a bundle of sticks and said, "Please give me the sticks to build a little house for myself." The man gave him the sticks and the pig built his house in one day.

Then along came the big bad wolf. He growled and said, "Little pig, little pig, let me come in."

"Not by the hair of my chinny chin chin."

"Then I'll huff and I'll puff and I'll blow your house in." So he huffed and he puffed and he puffed and he huffed and at last he blew the house down! The second little pig ran away to find his brothers.

The third little pig met a man with a load of bricks. "Please give me those bricks to build a house with," said the little pig. The man gave him the bricks. The little pig worked very hard for a whole week and he built a very sturdy house with the bricks. Just as he was moving in, his two brothers came running.

"The big bad wolf huffed and puffed," said the first little pig.

"He blew both of our houses down!" said the second little pig. "Now we have no place to live."

"Come in, I have room in my house," said the third little pig.

Soon the big bad wolf came along. He growled and said, "Little pig, little pig, let me come in."

"Not by the hair of my chinny chin chin."

"Then I'll huff, and I'll puff, and I'll blow your house in."

Well, he huffed and he puffed, and he huffed and he puffed, and he puffed and huffed, but he could not blow the house down.

The big bad wolf tried to trick the little pig. He said, "Little pig, I know where there is a nice field of turnips."

The little pig did not open the door, but he spoke loudly enough for the wolf to hear. "Where?" asked the little pig.

"Oh, in Mr. Smith's field. Let's go tomorrow and get some! I will come for you tomorrow morning. What do you think?"

"Thank you very much," said the little pig, "I will be ready. What time do you mean to go?"

"At six o'clock."

Well, the little pig and his brothers got up at five, and together they got the turnips before the wolf came. When the big bad wolf arrived he said, "Little pig, are you ready?"

The little pig did not open the door. Through the closed door he shouted, "I have already been to Mr. Smith's field. I have a nice pot of turnips cooking for dinner. Thanks for telling me about them."

"Oh, turnip greens!" growled the wolf, stamping his feet. Still, he tried to trick the little pig again. He said, "Little pig, I know where there is a nice apple tree."

"Where?" said the pig.

"Down in the green meadow," replied the wolf, "We could go together tomorrow morning and get some apples. How about five o'clock tomorrow?"

Well, the little pig and his brothers got up the next morning at four o'clock, and went off for the apples, hoping to get back before the wolf came. It was a long way, and they had to climb the tree. All three little pigs were still up in the tree when the wolf came running.

When the wolf came along he said, "Little pig! Are you here before me? I see you brought your brothers, too. Are they nice apples?"

"Yes, very," said the little pig. "I will throw you down one." And he threw it so far, that, while the wolf was gone to pick it up, the three little pigs jumped down and ran home with their baskets full of apples.

The next day the wolf came again, and said to the little pig, "Little pig, there is a fair in town this afternoon. Would you and your brothers like to go?"

"Oh yes," said the pig, "We will go. What time will you stop by for us?"

"At three," said the wolf. So the three little pigs went off early as usual. They went to the fair and bought a butter churn. When they were on their way home they saw the wolf coming. All three of them climbed into the butter churn to hide. It rolled down the hill with the pigs in it. The wolf jumped out of the way just in time. He was so scared that he ran home without going to the fair.

The next day he went to the little pig's house and saw the butter churn on the front steps. He knew he had been tricked. The wolf growled. "Turnip greens and apple stems! You rotten little pigs. I will eat you up, all three." He stamped his feet and shook his fist. "I will come down the chimney!"

When the little pigs heard the wolf climbing up on the roof, they were scared. The third little pig said to his brothers, "Quick, start a fire." Then he hung on the pot full of water. In no time the pot was hot and steamy. Just as the wolf was coming down, the third little pig took off the cover. His brothers huddled together across the room, shaking with fright.

Down, down, the chimney climbed the big bad wolf. He growled and said, "I will eat you up, one … by … one!" Just then the wolf slipped, and he fell with a splash into the steamy pot. The third little pig put on the cover. "He is trapped! We are saved!" he shouted. The three little pigs danced and played while the big bad wolf simmered in the pot.

Together the three little pigs took care of their cozy house of bricks. They planted a garden and worked very hard. They were never again bothered by the big bad wolf, and they lived happily ever after.

This story comes from England. Adapted from a story collected by Joseph Jacobs.

Three Little Pigs Finger Puppets

Directions

Copy the patterns for each child. You may cut them out, or suggest that parents do this at home. Have the children color them at story-time. Encourage parents to retell the story at home with their child, using the finger puppets.

 This craft takes 5 minutes to complete.

Dancing

Before Sharing Books

Put on some cheerful music and let the children dance freestyle for a few moments. Turn the music softer and softer, as you dance more slowly. Have the children sit down, but let their hands continue to dance. Finally, turn the music off and ask the children to put their hands in their lap. Everyone is now ready to hear stories.

Literacy Tip for Parents

While getting dressed in the morning, make up rhymes with your child about the clothes he or she is wearing—new blue shoe, better sweater, dance pants, a shirt with no dirt, etc.

Rhymes, Songs, and Fingerplays

Song

"Do Your Pants Like to Dance?" *Tune: "Do Your Ears Hang Low?"*
Linguistic Intelligence

Do your pants like to dance?
Do they wiggle and prance?
Do they make you laugh?
Do you call them fancy pants?
When you put them on each morning,
Do they wiggle without warning?
Do your pants like to dance?

(You may take a few minutes to talk about the rhyming words, and the words that start with "W.")

Rhyme

Dancing D
Linguistic Intelligence, Spatial Intelligence

Big D and Little D,
Dance day and night.
They dance to the left,
They dance to the right.
They dance in a circle,
They dance in a square.
They dance all the way,
To the county fair.

(Make stick puppets of upper- and lowercase "D," and make them dance while you recite the rhyme.)

Fingerplay

Dancing Fingers
Bodily-Kinesthetic Intelligence

Dancing pinkies.
(Wiggle little fingers on both hands.)
Dancing thumbs.
(Wiggle both thumbs.)
Look out tummy,
Here they come!
(Tickle your tummy.)

Rhymes

Bounce Rhymes for Infant Storytime

Cackle, cackle Mother Goose,
Have you any feathers loose?
Truly have I, pretty fellow,
Quite enough to fill a pillow.

If all the world were apple pie,
And all the sea were ink,
And all the trees were bread and cheese,
What would we have to drink?

Nursery Rhyme for Cultural Awareness
Linguistic Intelligence

Great A, little a,
Bouncing B,
The cat's in the cupboard,
And can't see me.

Books to Share

Appelt, Kathi. *Piggies in a Polka.* Harcourt, 2003. Pigs dance the night away when a polka band plays at the annual hootenanny.

Conover, Chris. *Over the Hills and Far Away.* Farrar, Straus and Giroux, 2004. A skillful piper makes people happy as he goes about playing music that lightens their burdens and makes them want to dance.

Spinelli, Eileen. *Three Pebbles and a Song.* Dial, 2003. As his mouse family endures a long, cold winter, Moses's contributions of a dance, a juggling act, and a little song prove more useful than he had supposed.

Stower, Adam. *Two Left Feet.* Bloomsbury Publishing, 2004. Rufus, a monster who has trouble dancing due to his two left feet, finds the perfect partner for the dance competition.

Wilson, Karma. *Hilda Must Be Dancing.* Simon & Schuster, 2004. Hilda Hippo tries other, quieter, activities when her jungle friends are disturbed by her dancing. But nothing else makes her happy until Water Buffalo suggests swimming and she finds a new way to express herself.

The Dancing Monkeys

Once upon a time, a prince lived in a castle. Day after day, he studied princely things. He was a good student, but how he wished for a little bit of fun!

"Please let me have some monkeys," he asked the king. So the king sent away for six monkeys, and in a little while, they arrived. The prince was playing with his monkeys one afternoon while the courtiers danced. All at once, the monkeys began to dance. The courtiers twirled, and the monkeys twirled. The courtiers stepped high, and the monkeys stepped high. So the prince began to train his monkeys to dance. He had costumes and hats made for them.

Soon the prince's dancing monkeys were performing every night after dinner for the king and queen. "Terrific. Outstanding. Excellent!" the king exclaimed.

Now one of the courtiers was jealous of the monkeys. "They are only dumb little animals," the courtier grumbled.

When festival days arrived, the prince took his monkeys into town to perform on a big stage. The king and queen attended, watching from their royal carriage. Many people came to see the show. Dressed in their fine costumes and hats, the monkeys took the stage. The monkeys twirled. The monkeys stepped high. They danced beautifully, and the people cheered.

"Long live the prince! Long live his dancers!" the people shouted.

The jealous courtier was watching, too. He was angry because the people loved the monkeys. "They never cheered like that for me," he mumbled. He reached into his pocket and took out some nuts. He threw the nuts onto the stage. All at once, the monkeys stopped dancing. They pulled off their hats. They scrambled across the stage, and fought one another for the nuts. The music played on, but the dancing was over.

The people laughed. The prince was embarrassed. He ran onto the stage, to collect his monkeys. He gathered them all, putting them on his shoulders, and on his back and on his head.

"Long live the prince!" the people shouted. "Long live his monkeys!" So the prince, with all of his monkeys, took a bow. The king and queen smiled. The jealous courtier, who thought he had spoiled everything, ran away.

Story based on one of Aesop's fables.

Dancing Monkeys Stick Puppet

Directions

Copy the pattern for each child and cut it out.
At storytime, have the children color the monkey, and then paste or tape it to a craft stick.
The children can now make their monkeys dance, while you play some cheerful music.

 This craft and music activity takes 10 minutes to complete.

Dinner

Before Sharing Books

Bring some place setting items and ask the children to help you set the table correctly. First lay out a tablecloth or place mat. Give someone the plate, the napkin, the spoon, and the other pieces and let him or her set the items on the table. When the table is set, you and the children are ready for stories about dinner.

Literacy Tip for Parents

Teach your child that reading is important to you. Let him or her see you opening your mail, reading the newspaper, or using a recipe to make dinner or a favorite treat.

Rhymes, Songs, and Fingerplays

Song

"ABC Dinner" *Tune: "Twinkle, Twinkle Little Star"*
Musical Intelligence and Letter Recognition

A for apple,
B for bread,
C for carrots, orange-red.
D for drink, here in my cup.
E for eat! Eat it up.
Dinner time is fun for me.
When I eat my ABC's.

Action Rhyme

I Like Dinner
Bodily-Kinesthetic Intelligence
(Rub tummy after each line.)

I like chicken.
I like peas.
I like bread,
And cottage cheese.
I like soup with
Cracker crumbs.
I like dinner.
Give me some!

Rhymes

Bounce Rhymes for Infant Storytime

Curly Locks, Curly Locks,
Will you be mine?
You shall not wash dishes.
Nor yet feed the swine,
But sit on a cushion.
And sew a fine seam.
And feed upon strawberries,
Sugar, and cream.

The lion and the unicorn.
Were fighting for the crown.
The lion beat the unicorn.
And all around the town.
Some gave them white bread.
And some gave them brown.
Some gave them plum cake.
And sent them out of town.

Nursery Rhyme for Cultural Awareness

Jack Sprat could eat no fat.
His wife could eat no lean.
And so betwixt the two of them,
They licked the platter clean.

Books to Share

Cooke, Trish. *Full, Full, Full of Love.* Candlewick Press, 2003. For young Jay Jay, Sunday dinner at Gran's house is full of hugs and kisses, tasty dishes, all kinds of fishes, happy faces, and love.

Cuyler, Margery. *Please Say Please!* Scholastic, 2004. Penguin teaches his animal friends how to behave when they are invited for dinner.

Kasza, Keiko. *My Lucky Day.* Penguin, 2003. When a young pig knocks on a fox's door, the fox thinks dinner has arrived, but the pig has other plans.

Rylant, Cynthia. *Little Whistle's Dinner Party.* Harcourt, 2001. A guinea pig who lives in Toytown invites his friends in the toy store to a dinner party at midnight.

Spinelli, Eileen. *Night Shift Daddy.* Hyperion, 2000. A father shares dinner and bedtime rituals with his daughter before going out to work the night shift.

Stone Soup

Many years ago three tired and hungry soldiers came upon a small village. War had been hard on the villagers. The harvest that year was very small and the people had almost nothing to eat. What food they had, they hid away so no one could find it. When the soldiers asked people in the square for a meal, no one offered to feed them.

The soldiers spoke quietly among themselves. Then the first soldier spoke to the crowd in the square. "Your tired fields have left you nothing to share, so we will share what little we have. We will share the secret of how to make soup from a stone." The soldier then pulled from his breast pocket, a smooth white stone. He held it in the palm of his hand for all to see. A little boy touched the stone and called, "Soup from a stone? How can it be?" Soon many people gathered around to see.

The soldiers built a fire in the village square. They borrowed a large pot and filled it with clean springwater. The villagers watched every move as the soldiers worked. They held their breath as the stone was dropped into the steaming pot.

"This will be a fine soup," said the second soldier as he stirred the pot. "If we had a pinch of salt it would be wonderful!"

A woman in a blue scarf stood up and said, "I know where to find some salt." When she returned, she had the salt, and some parsley and an onion in her apron. All of these were added to the pot. In a short time, it smelled delicious.

"Soup from a stone! You soon will see," called the tired travelers three.

One by one, the men and women of the village remembered where to find barley, carrots, and even a bit of beef. Just before the soldiers were ready to serve the soup, a few loaves of bread and some sweet butter appeared. Tables and chairs were brought to the square for the feast. Every man, woman, and child was served a bowl of soup before the soldiers ate. Everyone ate to their satisfaction.

Musical instruments were brought out from the attics and barns. They ate and danced and sang well into the night. The fear that had gripped this village for so long was, for the moment, completely dispelled.

In the morning the three soldiers awoke to find every person of the village standing before them. At their feet lay a satchel of bread and cheese.

"You have given us a great gift," said an old man. "You shared the secret of how to make soup from stones." The soldiers smiled. The third soldier said, "Soup from a stone, prepared by neighbors. It's the sharing that gives it flavor."

The soldiers picked up the satchel of food. Smiling and waving good-bye to their new friends, they walked down the road.

Traditional French folktale.

Stone Soup Coloring Sheet

Directions
Copy the picture for each child. Have them color it with crayons or markers.

 This craft takes 5 minutes to complete.

Feet

Before Sharing Books

Play a guessing game with the children. Give them clues such as: I have two of these, sometimes they are cold, I need them when I ride a bike, I need them when I dance, etc.

Literacy Tip for Parents

Telling stories to your child is fun. It also helps him or her learn new vocabulary words and the structure of stories.

Rhymes, Songs, and Fingerplays

Song

"We Are Walking"
Tune: "Frére Jacques"
Musical Intelligence and Bodily-Kinesthetic Intelligence

We are walking.
We are walking.
Now we hop.
Now we hop.
Running, running, running.
Running, running, running.
Now let's stop.
Now let's stop.

Action Rhyme

Two Little Feet
Musical-Rhythmic Intelligence and Bodily-Kinesthetic Intelligence

I have two little feet.
Here's what they can do.
They can run very fast!
They can tiptoe, too.
They can stomp. They can tap.
Or twirl me in the air.
Socks and shoes,
Are what they wear.

Rhymes

How Many Feet?
Logical-Mathematical Intelligence and Naturalist Intelligence

Birds have two.
Dogs have four.
Spiders have eight!
That's quite a lot more.

Bounce Rhymes for Infant Storytime

Shoe the old horse,
Shoe the old mare.
But let the little ponies run,
Bare, bare, bare.

Father and Mother
And Uncle John,
Went to market one by one.
Father fell off ___!
And Mother fell off ____!
But Uncle John,
Went on, and on,
And on, and on …

(Bounce the child on your lap while saying this rhyme. Dip the child when you say "Father fell off and Mother fell off," then bounce faster when you say "on and on and on.")

Nursery Rhyme for Cultural Awareness

This little piggy went to market.
This little piggy stayed home.
This little piggy ate roast beef.
This little piggy had none.
And this little piggy cried
"Wee Wee Wee" all the way home.

(Say this rhyme while touching and wiggling toes one by one.)

Books to Share

Devine, Monica. *Carry Me, Mama.* Fitzhenry & Whiteside, 2005. Mama knows that Katie is now old enough to walk by herself, instead of being carried. Gently, she persuades her reluctant child to walk the stone's throw to Aunt Nina's house. Next, she takes the girl to Uncle Kalila's cabin, "as far as a rabbit runs." After gradually increasing the distance of their walks, the mother finds that her daughter is soon able to go "as far as a raven flies."

Griffin, Kitty. *The Foot-Stomping Adventures of Clementine Sweet.* Houghton Mifflin, 2004. When her family ignores her on her sixth birthday, Clementine gets mad and starts stomping on people with her very strong legs and super tough feet, but a tangle with a tornado turns things around for her.

Hess, Nina. *Whose Feet?* Random House, 2004. Introduces feet and describes how their differences allow animals to do special things, such as a mole's long, thick claws that are made for digging, and a bat's strong feet that can hook into rocks.

Ross, Tony. *Centipede's 100 Shoes.* Henry Holt & Company, 2003. A little centipede buys shoes to protect his feet but finds that they are a lot of trouble to put on and take off.

Winter, Rick. *Dirty Birdy Feet.* Rising Moon, 2000. A family's dinnertime is disrupted when a bird flies down the chimney, starting a wild chase across the newly cleaned carpet.

The Race of Tortoise and Hare

Once there was a hare that was very proud of his speed. To every creature he met he bragged, "My feet, my feet, are swift and sweet! No one can ever beat my feet!"

It so happened that the animals were having a fair. All of the animals came to enjoy the games and the food. When the hare learned that there was to be a race at the fair, he bragged to everyone, "My feet, my feet, are swift and sweet! No one can ever beat my feet!"

Because of this, not one creature signed up for the race. The hare laughed and laughed. "Ha! No one will race against me. I win!"

The tortoise said quietly, "I accept your challenge. I will race you."

"You must be joking," said the hare.

"Everyone wants to see a race. Race me. You do want to prove that you are fast, right?"

"My feet, my feet, are swift and sweet! No one can ever beat my feet!" said the hare. "It's a race."

The course for the race was a mile, along a road that circled through some trees and through a stream. The finish line was in a sunny field. As soon as the race began, the animals crowded at the finish line.

From the start, the hare was ahead. He ran along the road saying, "My feet, my feet, are swift and sweet! No one can ever beat my feet!" He ran until he came to the trees. "I know the tortoise is way behind me. I'll just take a nap under this shady tree, and then I will dash to the finish line and listen to everybody cheer!"

The tortoise just put one foot in front of the other. He wasn't fast, but he kept going. He followed the road until he came to the trees. There he saw the rabbit curled up in the shade, fast asleep. The tortoise put one foot in front of the other. One foot in front of the other. He swam across the stream, and then kept on walking. One foot in front of the other.

When the hare awoke from his nap, he stretched and yawned. He turned his head and looked toward the finish line.

"What? How can that be?" he said, jumping to his feet. "My feet, my feet, are swift and sweet! No one can ever beat my feet!" The hare ran as fast as he could for the finish line, but he could not catch up in time to save the race. The tortoise crossed ahead of him. All the animals cheered for the tortoise. He was the star of the fair.

"How did you do that?" asked the hare.

"I'm slow and steady," said the tortoise, "just slow … and … steady."

Retold from Aesop's fable.

Caterpillar's Shoes

Directions
Copy the pattern for each child and cut out the shoes. Have them paste the last two shoes on the caterpillar's feet with a glue stick. They may also color the picture.

 This craft takes 10 minutes to complete.

Foxes

Before Sharing Books

Bring several items that rhyme with fox. Ask the children to guess the animal whose name rhymes with these things. Suggestions: socks, blocks, box, locks, rocks.

Literacy Tip for Parents

Studies show that hearing language actually changes the structure of a baby's brain. Language builds more connections between neurons in the brain, so the more you talk with your baby, the more connections he will have in his brain.

Rhymes, Songs, and Fingerplays

Fingerplay

I Am the Fox

Bodily-Kinesthetic Intelligence, Naturalist Intelligence
I have two pointy ears on top of my head.
(Hands on head.)
I am covered with soft fur, rich and red. (*Brush shoulder with hand.*)
I have a bushy tail with a bright white tip.
(Pretend to stroke your tail.)
I am very tricky, clever, and quick. *(Touch forehead.)*
I am the Fox! You better watch out. *(Shake finger.)*
I will snatch your chickens and pop them in my mouth! *(Hand to mouth.)*

Song

"Does a Fox Wear Socks?" *Tune: "Do Your Ears Hang Low?"*
Musical-Rhythmic Intelligence
Does a fox wear socks?
Can he catch the chicken pox?
Does he like to play checkers,
Does he like to play with blocks?
Is he very tricky?
Are his paws always sticky?
Does a fox wear socks?

Action Rhyme

Big Fox, Little Fox

Bodily-Kinesthetic Intelligence
Big fox, little fox, *(Hold your hand head high, then knee high.)*
On a summer night.
Ran through the yard, *(Run in place very fast!)*
And gave the farmer's wife a fright.

Big fox, little fox, *(Hold your hand head high, then knee high.)*
Early in the morn,
Big yawn, little yawn, *(Yawn twice.)*
Asleep in the corn. *(Lay head on hands, pretend to sleep.)*

Rhymes

Bounce Rhyme for Infant Storytime
The fox went out one stormy night,
Prayed for the moon to give him light,
For he had many miles to travel that night,
Before he reached the town-o, town-o, town-o.
He had many miles to travel that night,
Before he reached the town-o.

Nursery Rhyme for Cultural Awareness
A-hunting we will go,
A-hunting we will go,
We'll catch a little fox,
And put him in a box,
And then we'll let him go!

Books to Share

Gray, Kes. *Cluck O'Clock.* Holiday House, 2004. A group of chickens has a full day on the farm, from eating breakfast early in the morning to avoiding a fox late at night.

Hindley, Judy. *Do Like a Duck Does!* Candlewick Press, 2002. By challenging a hairy stranger to imitate the behavior of herself and her ducklings, a mother duck proves the stranger is a fox and not a duck.

Jones, Carol. *The Gingerbread Man.* Houghton Mifflin, 2002. A freshly baked gingerbread man escapes when he is taken out of the oven and eludes a series of nursery rhyme characters who hope to eat him until meeting up with a clever fox.

McBratney, Sam. *I'll Always Be Your Friend.* HarperCollins, 2001. A little fox gets angry and tells his mother, "I'm not your friend anymore," when she tells him it's time to stop playing.

Ruhmann, Karl. *The Fox and the Stork: A Fable by Aesop.* North-South Books, 2003. When sly Fox invites hungry Stork to lunch but tricks her out of her portion, she devises a way to get the last laugh.

The Fox and the Goat

One day, a fox fell into a well. He tried and tried to climb out, but it was much too deep. The fox sighed, "Oh, how will I ever get out?"

Later that day, a goat came along. The goat was very thirsty, so he looked down the well. Was he surprised to see a fox way down there!

"Hello, friend. Is the water any good?" called the goat to the fox.

"I must say it is the best! This water is cool and fresh and delicious!" answered the fox. "Why don't you come down and try some?"

Without thinking about how he would get out again, the goat jumped into the well. He took a long, cool drink! The water was very good, just as the fox had said it would be.

"Well, my friend, we are in trouble," said the fox. This well is very deep. I have tried over and over to climb out on my own, but I cannot do it."

"What are we to do?" asked the goat.

"Don't worry. I have an idea," said the fox. "If you place your forefeet up on the wall and bend your head, I will run up your back and escape. Once I am out, I will help you." So the goat did just as the fox asked. The fox leaped on his back, climbed onto the goat's head, steadied himself on the goat's horns, and climbed to safety.

"Good-bye," said the fox.

"Don't go. You promised to help me!" cried the goat. "You must!"

"If you had as many brains in your head as you have hairs in your beard, you would not be in trouble, my friend. You should not have jumped into the well without a plan for getting back up." The fox ran away, laughing. He left the goat in the well.

If the goat got out, well, he is smarter than the fox believed him to be. If he did not, he serves as a warning to others. Look before you leap.

Adapted from Aesop's fable.

Big Fox and Little Fox Finger Puppets

Directions

Copy the patterns for each child and cut them out. Have the children color them with markers or crayons. They may put their fingers through the holes, making the legs for Big Fox and Little Fox. Encourage them to retell the Big Fox and Little Fox rhyme at home using the finger puppets.

 This craft takes 5 minutes to complete.

Friends

Before Sharing Books

Display some stuffed animal toys. Talk about some activities that these "friends" enjoy doing together, such as chasing butterflies, playing with a ball, and having lunch together.

Literacy Tip for Parents

It is okay to read the same book to your child many times. Children love familiar books, and the repetition helps them begin to recognize words and predict what comes next in a story.

Rhymes, Songs, and Fingerplays

Song

"Friend Song"
Tune: "My Bonnie Lies Over the Ocean"
Musical-Rhythmic Intelligence

A friend is someone you can play with.
A friend helps you pick up your toys.
A friend likes to laugh and share.
Friends can be girls or boys.
My friend, my friend.
I'm happy to call you my friend, my friend.
My friend, my friend.
I'm glad you are my friend, my friend.

(Repeat the song, and ask the children to raise their hand each time they hear the word "friend.")

Action Rhymes

Big F and Little F
Bodily-Kinesthetic Intelligence
(Literacy short story to act out.)

Big **F** and little **f** went out to play.
They climbed a hill and looked **f**ar away.
They saw some **f**luffy clouds **f**lying high!
They jumped three times. They tried to **f**ly.

They pretended to be a **f**ierce tiger cat.
"Roar! Roar! Roar! We're **f**ierce and we're **f**at!"
"I am getting hungry," little **f** said.
So they ran home for lunch, **f**resh **f**ruit and brown bread.

(Make Big F and little f stick figures on short dowels, soda straws or pencils. Hold them up each time you say the sound "f.")

Rhyme

Bounce Rhymes for Infant Storytime

Bum Bum Bailey-o.
Two to one, the barble-o.
Barble-o, barble-o.
Bum Bum Bailey-o.

Ride a cockhorse to Banbury Cross,
To see a fine lady on a white horse.
Rings on her fingers and bells on her toes,
She shall have music wherever she goes.

Nursery Rhyme for Cultural Awareness

Jack and Jill went up the hill,
To fetch a pail of water.
Jack fell down and broke his crown,
And Jill came tumbling after.

Books to Share

Austin, Margot. *A Friend for Growl Bear.* HarperCollins, 1999. None of the animals in the forest will play with the little bear who growls all the time, until Old Owl realizes that the little bear is not trying to scare anyone, he just has not yet learned to talk.

Beaumont, Karen. *Being Friends.* Dial, 2002. Two very different girls learn to appreciate each other and discover the joy of being friends. Rhyming text is playful.

Bottner, Barbara. *Rosa's Room.* Peachtree Publishers, 2004. Rosa's new room in her new house seems empty, even with the decorations she has arranged in it. Then Rosa adds something new, and her new room is just right.

Carlson, Nancy. *How About A Hug?* Viking, 2001. There are many occasions that call for a hug, and a hug that is just right for each one.

Crimi, Carolyn. *Don't Need Friends.* Random House, 1999. After his best friend moves away from the junkyard, Rat decides he doesn't need friends, until he and a grouchy dog decide that they need each other.

The Little Red Hen

Once there was a Little Red Hen who had ten hungry chicks. One day, the Little Red Hen found a kernel of wheat. "Hurray!" said the Little Red Hen. "This wheat will grow."

The Little Red Hen asked her friends for help, "Who will help me plant the wheat?"

The cat said, "I won't."

The pig said, "I won't."

The dog said, "No way! I won't. I won't. I won't."

"Okay," said the Little Red Hen. "Then I will plant the wheat myself." And she did.

When the wheat grew tall and turned golden, the Little Red Hen knew it was time to pick the wheat. She asked her friends for help.

"Who will help me pick the wheat?"

The cat said, "I won't."

The pig said, "I won't."

The dog said, "No way! I won't. I won't. I won't."

"Okay," said the Little Red Hen. "Then I will pick it myself." And she did. Now the Little Red Hen wanted to take the sacks of wheat to the mill, so it could be ground into soft, white flour. She asked her friends for help.

"Who will help me take the wheat to the mill?"

The cat said, "I won't."

The pig said, "I won't."

The dog said, "No way! I won't. I won't. I won't."

"Okay," said the Little Red Hen. I will take it myself, in my wagon. And she did. Then the Little Red Hen was ready to bake bread from the flour. She asked her friends for help.

"Who will help me bake some bread?"

The cat said, "I won't."

The pig said, "I won't."

The dog said, "No way! I won't. I won't. I won't."

"Okay," said the Little Red Hen. "I will bake the bread myself." And she did. She mixed some milk, some flour, some oil, and some yeast in a bowl until she had a soft dough. She put the dough in a warm place and the dough grew bigger and bigger and bigger. When the bread was ready to bake, she put it in the hot oven and closed the door. Soon, her four friends came over. They could smell the delicious bread baking.

The Little Red Hen took the bread out of the oven. "Who will help me eat this bread?"

The cat said, "ME!"

The pig said, "ME!"

The dog said, "ME, ME, ME!"

"No way!" said the Little Red Hen. "You won't. You won't. You won't. My hungry chicks and I will eat the bread." And they did.

Storytelling Tips: *Children may enjoy joining in on the responses for the cat, the pig, and the dog. You may like to use flannel board figures, puppets, or masks to add visual interest. Mime with the children mixing the bread dough. After telling the story, ask the children what would happen if the cat, the pig, and the dog did help the Little Red Hen. You may want to bring some home baked bread to share.*

This story comes from England. Adapted from a story collected by Joseph Jacobs.

Friendly Faces

Directions

Copy the face pieces for each child and cut them out. Give each child a 6" paper plate and a glue stick. Allow them to make Friendly Faces by gluing on the face pieces. They may also like to color them with crayons or markers.

 This craft takes 5 minutes to complete.

Getting Dressed

Before Sharing Books

Display a variety of shoes, socks, hats, sweaters, etc. Using yourself or a puppet for a model, try these items on, but put them on incorrectly. Put the socks on your hands, for example. Let the children tell you the correct way to put on the clothes.

Literacy Tip for Parents

Try serving a meal of foods that begin with a single letter sound—bananas, beets, and beef; tomatoes, turkey, and tangerines; carrots, cantaloupe, and cottage cheese. Talk about the letter sounds while you eat.

Rhymes, Songs, and Fingerplays

Song

"Hat, Sweater, Pants, and Boots"
Tune: "Head, Shoulders, Knees, and Toes"
Musical-Rhythmic Intelligence and
Bodily-Kinesthetic Intelligence

Hat, sweater, pants and boots, pants and boots.
Hat, sweater, pants and boots, pants and boots.
I get dressed and look so cute!
Hats, sweater, pants and boots, pants and boots.

(As you sing the song, touch the appropriate parts of the body. Put hands by face and smile when you sing "look so cute.")

Action Rhyme and Flannel Board Activity

Silly Sandy
Bodily-Kinesthetic Intelligence

Silly Sandy, get dressed today!
Your friends are waiting. They want to play.
You can't go out in your underwear!
Put on your shirt. It goes right ... here.

For action rhyme, touch your foot first, then your chest when you say "shirt." Repeat with assorted items of clothing: pants, socks, jacket, etc. Use the craft pattern on page 56 to create a flannel board or magnetic board activity for Silly Sandy.

Rhymes

Bounce Rhymes for Infant Storytime

Cobbler, cobbler, mend my shoe.
Get it done by half-past two.
Stitch it up and stitch it down,
Then I'll give you half a crown.

Whose little pigs are these, these, these?
Whose little pigs are these?
They are Rogers and Cooks.
I know by their looks.
I found them among my peas.
(Touch baby's toes when you say "Whose little pigs are these?")

Nursery Rhyme for Cultural Awareness

Baa, baa, black sheep.
Have you any wool?
Yes sir, yes sir,
Three bags full.
One for my master,
And one for the dame,
And one for the little boy,
Who lives down the lane.

Books to Share

Arnold, Tedd. *Huggly Gets Dressed.* Scholastic, 1998. A monster from under the bed tries to wear people clothes, but he ends up wearing mittens on his toes and underwear on his head.

Chodos-Irvine, Margaret. *Ella Sarah Gets Dressed.* Harcourt, 2003. Ella Sarah wants to wear an unusual and colorful outfit of her own choosing, not the sensible ones others recommend. This is a good book for discussing colors. Caldecott Honor Book.

Fleming, Candace. *This Is the Baby.* Farrar, Straus and Giroux, 2004. In this cumulative story in rhyme, all of the items of clothing are listed that go on a baby who hates to get dressed.

Mould, Wendy. *Ants In My Pants.* Clarion Books, 2001. Mother wants Jacob to put on clothes to go shopping, but he wants to stay home and play. He describes imaginary animals that are keeping him from dressing. Rhymes include ants in my pants, fox in my socks, geese in my fleece, and more.

Spinelli, Eileen. *In My New Yellow Shirt.* Henry Holt & Company, 2001. A boy wears his new yellow shirt and is transformed in his imagination into a duck, a lion, a daffodil, a trumpet, and other things.

Eat, My Clothes!

Giufa worked at the food shop. He swept the floors. He polished the windows. He kept the vegetables and fruits nice and neat. This he did cheerfully and well, but no one ever thanked him.

Nobody in town liked Giufa. The dogs barked at him. The women laughed at him. The children were told not to talk to him. This was because Giufa was ragged and poor.

One evening, after working all day at the food shop, Giufa delivered milk and eggs to a rich man's house. The rich man had guests at his house for dinner. Giufa could smell the roasted chickens and fresh bread. His stomach growled!

The rich man grabbed the milk and eggs and said, "Go away, Giufa! You are too ragged and dirty to be seen by my fine dinner guests." Then the rich man called his dogs and told them to chase Giufa away.

When he got home that night, with tears in his eyes, Giufa told his mother about being so badly treated at the rich man's house.

"Don't be sad, my son," she said. "You will soon be welcomed to his house."

That night, she went to the rich man's home. She found a coat, a velvet vest, and some pants hanging on the clothesline. She found a fine hat and a pair of boots near the back door. "I will borrow these," she said. "Then we shall see what we shall see."

In the morning, Giufa put on the fine clothes that his mother gave him. He walked down the street towards the food shop. Women waved and said good morning! Children sang and danced about him, and they gave him warm bread and fruit. The dogs did not bark or chase him. "What a fine day I am having," said Giufa.

The rich man came walking down the street toward Giufa. He shook his hand and said, "Good morning, sir. Welcome to our village." Then he invited Giufa to his home for dinner that night.

Dressed in fine clothes, Giufa arrived at the rich man's home. With great ceremonies, he was greeted and seated at the table. Many fine dishes were served to him. Giufa ate the delicious food until his stomach was full. Then he put the food that was left into his pockets, his hat and his shoes.

"Eat, my clothes," he said. "You were invited to dinner tonight, not I."

Italian folktale, retold.

One, Two! Put On Your Shoes!

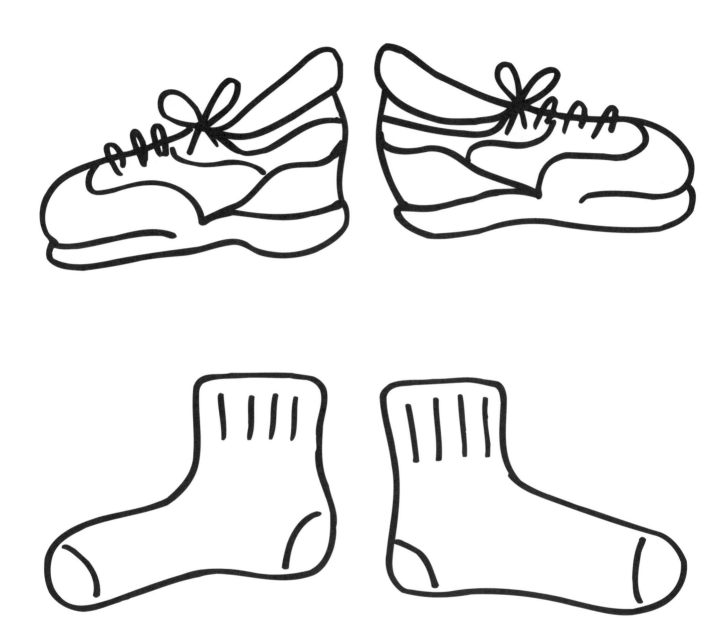

Directions
Copy the shoe and sock patterns for each child and cut them out. At storytime, have the children paste the shoes over the socks, using a glue stick.

 This craft takes 10 minutes to complete.

Silly Sandy Patterns

Directions

Copy the Silly Sandy paper doll and clothing for each child and cut them out. Allow the children to dress Silly Sandy by gluing on clothing with a glue stick. They may also wish to color the doll and clothing. Be sure to show the children the "S" in Silly and Sandy, to increase their letter recognition skills.

 This craft takes 5 to 10 minutes to complete.

Home

Before Sharing Books

How do you know when you are home? Give some ideas, and ask the children, too. Here are some ideas: I am home when my key fits in the door, when someone who loves me says hello, when I know just where to find a snack, when my favorite toy is just where I thought it would be.

Literacy Tip for Parents

Music helps your child develop mathematical intelligence. Clapping rhythms, learning to sing a tune, and playing an instrument help your child learn to count and understand fractions. Listening to classical music can also improve memory and reduce stress.

Rhymes, Songs, and Fingerplays

Song

"Home Again"
Tune: "Row, Row, Row Your Boat"
Musical-Rhythmic Intelligence

Home, home, home again,
After school or play.
Home is where I want to be,
At the end of day.

(You may repeat the song, and ask the children to clap the rhythm as you sing.)

Action Story

Hide-away Home: Story Featuring the Letter H
Letter Recognition
(You may want to draw a letter "H" on thumb with a pen before telling this story.)

Henry had a habit of hiding.
(Hold up thumb for Henry the Mouse.)
He hid under bushes.
(Cover thumb with palm of the other hand.)
He hid in the grass.
(Wiggle fingers of other hand in front of thumb.)
He hid under crumpled napkins and paper cups.
(Cup hand over thumb.)
Henry hid anywhere he could.
(Tuck thumb behind ear, in sleeve, etc.)
But Henry never had a home of his own.
(Sigh and look sad.)
However, Henry had determination!

When Henry decided he wanted a home,
He hunted for one!
(Turn thumb left and right, as if looking around.)
He hunted high!
(Thumb on head.)
He hunted low.
(Thumb under shoe.)
He hunted hither and yon!
(Thumb on a child's head, under a child's hand, etc.)
All of those places were good,
but Henry still hunted.
He wanted a good home.
He wanted a warm home.
He wanted a safe home.
He wanted a home that fit him just right.
It was nearly dark when Henry found … a hole!
(Curl hand into a loose fist.)
It was good, and warm, and safe,
and it fit him just right.
(Tuck thumb into fist.)
No more hiding for Henry.
Now Henry has a home.

Action Rhymes

Bounce Rhymes for Infant Storytime

Ladybug! Ladybug!
Fly away home.
Your house is on fire.
And your children all gone.

Little Bo Peep has lost her sheep,
And can't tell where to find them.
Leave them alone, and they will come home,
Wagging their tails behind them.

Nursery Rhyme for Cultural Awareness
This little piggy went to market.
This little piggy stayed home.
This little piggy ate roast beef,
This little piggy had none.
And this little piggy cried
"Wee, wee, wee" all the way home.

Books to Share

Briers, Erica. *Little Duck Lost.* Penguin, 2004. Little Duck is lost and asks the other animals to help him find his home.

Harper, Jessica. *I Like Where I Am.* Penguin, 2004. The rhyming story of a six-year-old boy who is sad about moving to a new home but ends up being happy when he gets there.

Hutchins, Pat. *Don't Get Lost!* Greenwillow Books, 2004. When Little Piglet, Little Lamb, Little Calf, and Little Foal take a walk across the fields after breakfast, they seem to lose their way as they try to head for home.

Lin, Grace. *Robert's Snow.* Penguin, 2004. Robert, a little mouse anxious to experience snow, falls out of his bedroom window in his family's boot home and has a snow adventure.

Whybrow, Ian. *The Noisy Way to Bed.* Scholastic, 2004. As a sleepy boy decides it is bedtime and sets out across the farm toward home, he meets several animals who, in their noisy way, express the same idea.

The Peddler of Swaffham

There was a certain man who lived in the town of Swaffham. He had a little cottage with an orchard in back. He was a peddler by trade and he sold thread and pots and soap and other useful things which he carried in a pack. He made a little money, but for sure he was far from rich.

One night he had a dream. In the dream he saw a yellow cat. The cat stood on its hind legs and said, plain as can be, "Go to London Bridge and you'll hear good news." In the morning the peddler shook his head and said to himself, "I'd be a fool to believe a talking cat!"

He thought no more about the dream all day. But that night, he dreamed the same dream again. A yellow cat stood up and said, "Go to London Bridge and you'll hear good news." In the morning the peddler soaked his head in cold water, to bring himself to his senses! Talking cat! Who ever heard of that?

But for the third night in a row, the peddler dreamed of a yellow cat. The cat stood up and began to speak. But the peddler quickly said to the cat, "I'll go to London Bridge, since you have gone to all this trouble to visit me three nights in a row."

The next morning, even before breakfast, the peddler started off, and in a few hours he made his way to London. He found London Bridge and walked right to the center of it. People passed him all day long. Not one person had any news for him, good or bad. When it grew dark, he wrapped his cloak about him and slept on the bridge. He was too uncomfortable to dream! He waited there all the next day, and still no one had any news for him. After another cold night, the peddler woke up stiff and hungry.

"That's what I get for listening to a yellow cat!" he said to himself. "He brushed off his trousers and put his hat on his head. He put his pack on his shoulders. He was about to go home to Swaffham, when someone spoke to him. It was the first person to speak to him since he came to London.

"What are you about, sir?" said the man. "That is my shop just there. I have watched you standing on this bridge for days now. It is clear to me that you are a peddler, yet you have not sold anything!"

"I am a peddler, and a dreamer," the peddler sighed. "Three nights in a row, I dreamed the same dream. A yellow cat told me to go to London Bridge. He said I would hear good news!"

"Dreams, dreams. There's no use chasing dreams," said the shopkeeper. He laughed a good long time. "I had a dream last night myself. I dreamed I was in Swaffham. I have never been to this place before. I saw an orchard next to a peddlers cottage. There was a large oak tree with a twisted branch growing there. I dug under the tree and found a great treasure! What a fool I would be to go off to Swaffham looking for that! You should go home, man."

The peddler smiled. He shook the shopkeeper's hand. "Thank you, sir. I am going to do exactly as you suggest."

The peddler made his way home. He went to his orchard, and found the tree with the twisted branch. He dug under the tree and found a chest full of gold coins and jewels. Just as he opened the chest, a yellow cat walked by. From that day on, the yellow cat lived with the peddler. They lived in comfort all their days. The peddler was generous and kind to people in need and he gave a good bit of money to repair the Swaffham church. If you go to Swaffham, you will see a statue there in front of the church, of a smiling peddler carrying a pack.

Traditional folktale from England.

"Home Sweet Home" Sign

Directions

Copy the patterns and cut them out. Cut poster
board for each child, 12" x 6". At storytime,
have the children paste the phrase "Home
Sweet Home" and the house picture on the
poster board.

 **This craft takes 10 minutes
to complete.**

Lizards and Snakes

Before Sharing Books

Ask a pet store to allow you to borrow a chameleon or some other small lizard to display in a glass cage at your storytime. A live animal is always a big attraction! If you cannot obtain a live animal, display toy lizards or snakes. Ask the children to pretend that they are crawling up on a rock to bask in the sunshine, as a lizard or snake would do. As soon as they are settled in on their sunny spot, they are ready to hear stories.

Literacy Tip for Parents

At bedtime, create a story with your child about your child's day. "Mandy got up early. She played ball with Socks. She went shopping with Mom. She gave Daddy a kiss. She ate soup for dinner. Mandy had a good day."

Rhymes, Songs, and Fingerplays

Song

"Do You Have a Rattle Tail?"
Musical-Rhythmic Intelligence

Do you have a rattle tail,
A rattle tail, a rattle tail?
Do you have a rattle tail,
That shakes and shakes like this?

Yes I have a rattle tail,
A rattle tail, a rattle tail.
Yes I have a rattle tail.
I shake it while I hiss.

(Shake fist while singing, then at the end give a loud hiss!)

Action Rhymes

Leaping Lizards (Letter L)
Letter Sound Recognition,
Bodily-Kinesthetic Intelligence

One little lizard, lying very still.
(Place one hand on the other.)
Listens for the hoot-owl up on the hill.
(Put hand near ear.)
The owl says "Whoo—I see you."
(Make circles with index fingers and thumbs, and put over eyes.)
Leaping Lizards! Look at him go!
(Raise both hands over head and shake them.)

(Hint: Speak slowly and softly on the first three lines of rhyme, but on the last line speak fast with great excitement. Repeat the rhyme and ask the children to listen for the sound of the letter "L.")

Action Rhymes

Bounce Rhymes for Infant Storytime

What do you suppose?
A bee sat on my nose.
Then what do you think?
He gave me a wink,
And said, "I beg your pardon,
I thought you were the garden."

See-saw, Margery Daw,
Johnny shall have a new master;
He shall have but a penny a day,
Because he can't go any faster.

Nursery Rhyme for Cultural Awareness

Jack be nimble, Jack be quick,
Jack jump over the candlestick.

Books to Share

Florian, Douglas. ***Lizards, Frogs, and Polliwogs: Poems and Paintings.*** Harcourt, 2001. "Toadally" hilarious reptile and amphibian poems.

Ireland, Karin. ***Don't Take Your Snake for a Stroll.*** Harcourt, 2003. In this cautionary tale, a boy is advised not to take his unusual pets anywhere—"Don't take your skunk on an airplane," "Don't take your moose to the movies," etc. His pig will make a slobbery mess, and the snake will terrorize the neighborhood.

Provencher, Rose-Marie. ***Slithery Jake.*** HarperCollins, 2004. When Sid brings a snake home for a pet, the snake escapes! The whole family frantically searches for the pet that may be slinking under the covers, sleeping in Grandpa's noodles, or hiding under the dog dish. The family decides to camp outside until the pet's hideaway is revealed.

Shannon, George. ***Lizard's Guest.*** HarperCollins, 2003. While dancing around, Lizard accidentally steps on Skunk's toes and then promises to take care of lazy Skunk until his foot is healed. (Also try *Lizard's Home* and *Lizard's Song* by the same author.)

Tews, Susan. ***Lizard Sees the World.*** Houghton Mifflin, 1997. A lizard sets out to climb to the place where the edge of the world meets the sky, so that he can look down and see the whole bowl that is the world.

The Boy and the Snake

One day a small boy walked down a dusty road, dragging a stick behind him. The stick made a sound like this—creeeech! It was a cheery sound, and the boy liked it a lot. He walked along and walked along minding his own business when another sound tickled his ear. It was oh so soft, and oh so sad.

"Help me, boy. Help me!"

The boy looked around. Along the side of the road he saw a rattlesnake trapped under a big old log. He dropped his stick and said, "Oh, my!" The boy knew better than to get close to a snake. He picked up his stick and started to walk away, dragging the stick behind him. The stick made a sound like this—creeeech!

But once more he heard the snake, sounding oh so pitiful and oh so sad.

"Help me, boy. Help me!"

The boy stopped and turned around. He took one step toward he snake. He got down real low to get a good look at the big old log. The boy said, "Looks like you are stuck for good, snake. I could never lift that big old log."

"You could … if you use your stick. Help me, boy."

So the boy poked the end of his stick under the big old log. He rolled a big rock close by, under his stick. He pushed on one end of the stick, and the other end of his stick lifted that big old log right off the snake. "Gotta go," said the boy. He knew better than to get close to the snake. He picked up his stick and walked away, dragging the stick behind him. The stick made a sound like this—creeeech!

But he got no more than three steps down the road when once again he heard the snake, sounding oh so miserable and oh so sad.

"Help me, boy. Help me."

"I already did!" insisted the boy. "I moved that big old log and set you free. I won't get close to you. I know better than that."

"But I've been under that log for so long," moaned the snake. "Now I am ccccold and ssssstiff!"

"I guess you'll warm up some time," said the boy.

"But I would be warm right away if you put me in your pocket," said the snake. "Help me boy."

"I know better than to pick up a snake," said the boy.

"You could show me to your friends," said the snake.

"See that you mind your manners," said the boy. He walked over to the snake and lifted him up with his stick. The snake did not bite.

"See, it is perfectly safe," said the snake.

The boy picked up the snake and curled him into his pocket. Then he picked up his stick and walked down the road, dragging his stick behind him. The stick made a sound like this—creeeech! After a bit, the snake poked his head out of the boy's pocket.

"I'm warm now, boy. This will do."

So the boy pulled the snake out of his pocket. He set him down on the road. Quick as lightning, the snake coiled up and bit the boy on the leg!

"Why, snake! What kind of thanks is that? I moved the big old log. I warmed you in my pocket. I put you down on the road nice and gentle. Why did you bite me?"

"Now boy," whispered the snake. "You told me yourself. You know better than to pick up a snake."

American folktale.

Leaping Lizard Bracelet

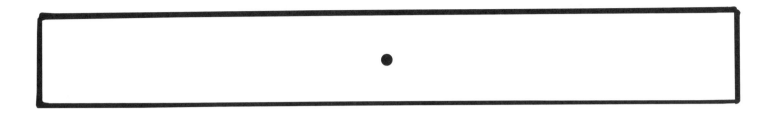

Directions

Copy the lizard pattern for each child and cut it out.
Tape the two 4" strips of paper together at a right
angle. Fold one strip over the other to make an accor-
dion spring. Attach the spring with tape to the 8" strip
of paper in the center (at the dot). At storytime, have
the children color their lizard with markers or crayons.
Attach the lizard to the paper spring with tape. Adjust
the paper strip to fit comfortable over the child's wrist
and attach with tape. When the child moves his or her
wrist the lizard will leap!

 **This craft takes 10 minutes
to complete.**

Morning

Before Sharing Books

Display a box of cereal, a comb, a newspaper, an alarm clock, and a lunch box. With a puppet or stuffed animal, show how each of these items is part of a typical morning routine.

Literacy Tip for Parents

Make up a story at breakfast, the sillier the better! The story should have a beginning, middle, and end. Anything can be a character, even the cereal spoon. "Spoonie went to the lake. He dove into the pool. He swam around and around and around. He found a golden treasure floating on the lake. He scooped it up. He took it to grandma's house. Grandma made it into a hat. 'Thank you, Grandma,' Spoonie said with a smile. That was Spoonie's favorite hat for a long, long time."

Rhymes, Songs, and Fingerplays

Song

"'T' Stands for Today"
Tune: "A Hunting We Will Go"
Letter Recognition, Musical Intelligence,
Interpersonal Intelligence

T stands for Today.
T stands for Today.
I hope you have a happy day.
T stands for Today.

T stands for Today.
T stands for Today.
Sing and smile and play awhile,
T stands for Today,

Action Rhyme

Early in the Morning
Bodily-Kinesthetic Intelligence

Early in the morning,
The sun comes up. *(Raise hands over head.)*
The dog jumps up. *(Raise hands over head.)*
The cat hops up. *(Raise hands over head.)*
The toast pops up. *(Raise hands over head.)*
And I get up! *(Stand up.)*

Song

"Bed Head"
Tune: "Twinkle Twinkle Little Star"
Musical-Rhythmic Intelligence

In the morning when I wake,
What a sight my hair can make!

It sticks up. It sticks out.
It's a tangled mess, no doubt.

Wet it, comb it, pat it flat.
I give up. I'll wear a hat!

Rhymes

Bounce Rhymes for Infant Storytime

Elsie Marley's grown so fine,
She won't get up to feed the swine.
But lies in bed till eight or nine.
Lazy Elsie Marley.

The cock's on the housetop, blowing his horn,
The bull's in the barn, a-threshing the corn,
The maids in the meadow are making the hay,
The ducks in the river are swimming away.

Nursery Rhyme for Cultural Awareness
It's raining.
It's pouring.
The old man is snoring.
He bumped his head
And went to bed
And he couldn't get up
In the morning.

Books to Share

Blos, Joan. *Hello, Shoes!* Simon & Schuster, 1999. A search for missing shoes provide a boy and his Grandpa opportunities to identify objects, name colors, and sing a song.

Edwards, Pamela Duncan. *The Grumpy Morning.* Hyperion, 1998. Whimsical rhyming story begins with a cow that moos for her morning milking, keeping the owl awake.

Gleeson, Libby. *Cuddle Time.* Candlewick Press, 2004. A little red-haired girl and her baby brother wake up early in the morning. They roll out of bed and crawl down the hall to their parent's room, which they call the monsters' cave.

McGee, Marni. *Wake Up, Me!* Simon & Schuster, 2002. A young child wakes up, greets the world, and gets ready to play.

Palatini, Margie. *Bedhead.* Simon & Schuster, 2000. Arthur has very unruly hair one morning. All the splashing and soaking and spraying aren't making it any better.

The Crows Are in the Corn

Once there was a pretty little farm, with chickens in the yard, a rooster in the barn, and a field of tall, yellow corn. The farmer and his wife, on this pretty little farm, worked hard every day and slept well every night. That's the way it was until one night.

On this night, the farmer brought a glass of milk and a wedge of cornbread to bed.

"My dear," said the farmer's wife, "you must not eat in bed. You'll get crumbs on the sheets and we won't sleep a wink!" But the farmer ate his snack in bed, anyway. When he was finished, he had crumbs in his beard. He had crumbs on his pajamas. He had crumbs on the sheets.

The farmer and his wife tossed and turned all night. At first light, the rooster crowed.

"Cock-a-doodle-doo! Wake up. Wake up."

Neither one of them wanted to get up. The farmer pulled the quilt up over his head. His wife covered her head with a pillow. They could not hear the rooster crow, and they went back to sleep.

Some crows were sitting in a tall oak tree that morning. When they noticed that no one was up, they quickly flew over to the corn field and started eating. They ripped open an ear of corn. They ate a few kernels and tossed the rest aside. Then they ripped open another ear. Oh, what a terrible mess they made.

"Caw-n, caw-n," they cackled excitedly as they ate their breakfast feast.

The rooster saw the crows. He did not like the mess they were making of the pretty corn. He crowed even louder. "Wake up, wake up, wake up!"

The farmer and his wife just kept sleeping, and the crows kept eating the corn. "Caw-n, caw-n," the crows called, as they continued their breakfast.

The rooster crowed even louder. "The crows are in the corn! The crows are in the corn!" The rooster cock-a-doodle-dooed with all his might.

The farmer kept snoring. His wife just rolled over.

The rooster was frantic. He tried once more, "The crows are in the corn. They're pulling up the corn!"

The farmer and his wife kept right on sleeping. And the crows kept right on eating. The rooster quit crowing in disgust. Nothing would wake the farmer and his wife. The chickens went out into the yard. Soon they came back and told the rooster, "The corn is all gone, all gone, all gone."

When the farmer and his wife finally rolled out of bed, they found their corn field picked clean and all torn up. From that day to this, farmers say "the crows are in the corn" when it is time to get up.

American folktale, southern states.

My Morning Wheel

Directions

Copy the pattern for each child and cut it out. At storytime, have the children color the pictures, then attach the circle to a paper plate with a brass brad. Tell the children that this wheel can help them remember to wash their face, comb their hair, put on their shoes, eat breakfast, brush their teeth, and give their parent or caregiver a kiss each morning.

 This craft takes 10 minutes to complete.

Music

Before Sharing Books

Bring two or three pieces of recorded music of different musical styles. Play each music selection, or a short part of it, and encourage the children to dance/move to show how the music makes them feel. Compare the three pieces of music and tell the children why you like them.

Literacy Tip for Parents

Clapping games help your child learn rhythm, and singing with your child helps him or her learn to hear and match pitch. You don't have to be a great singer to enjoy music. Just have fun!

Rhymes, Songs, and Fingerplays

Action Rhyme

I Make Music
Bodily-Kinesthetic Intelligence

I make music with my hands.
Listen while I clap.
Clap, Clap, Clap, Clap.
I really like to clap.

I make music with my feet.
Listen while I tap.
Tap, Tap, Tap, Tap.
I really like to tap.

I make music with my mouth.
Listen while I pop.
Pop, Pop, Pop, Pop.
I really like to pop. *(Put lips together, then open quickly to make a popping sound.)*

Song

"M U S I C"
Tune: "Row Row Row Your Boat"
Letter recognition,
Musical-Rhythmic Intelligence

Sing the melody through five times using the individual letter sounds for each syllable. The first time through the song, sing the "m" sound for each word. The second time through, sing a long "u" sound for each word. Continue using the letters in the word "music" until you've sung the song five times.

Suggestion: Display the letters from page 72 on a magnet board or flannel board, and point to the letters as you sing their sound.

Action Rhymes

Bounce Rhymes for Infant Storytime

Patty cake, patty cake,
Baker's man.
Bake me a cake just as fast as you can.
Roll it and pat it and mark it with a "B."
Then throw it in the oven for baby and me.

Humpty Dumpty sat on a wall.
Humpty Dumpty had a great fall.
All the king's horses and all the king's men,
Could not put Humpty together again.

Hey, diddle diddle,
The cat and the fiddle.
The cow jumped over the moon.
The little dog laughed to see such a sport
And the dish ran away with the spoon.

Nursery Rhyme for Cultural Awareness
(This rhyme may be spoken or sung.)

Jack and Jill went up the hill,
To fetch a pail of water.
Jack fell down and broke his crown,
And Jill came tumbling after.

Books to Share

Ajhar, Brian. *Home On the Range.* Dial, 2004. A young boy is transported, riding his rocking horse and wearing a cowboy hat, from a city apartment to life on the range.

London, Jonathan. *Who Bop?* HarperCollins, 2000. Hip hares and cool cats dance to the swinging music of Jazz-bo's saxophone.

Macken, JoAnn Early. *Sing-Along Song.* Penguin, 2004. From a robin chirping in the morning, to a lazy dog snoozing on the kitchen floor, to the sound of Daddy's home-at-last footsteps in the evening, the whole day rings with its own kind of music.

Rosenthal, Betsy. *My House Is Singing.* Harcourt, 2004. A collection of short poems about what's in a child's house. Subjects include the piano, the laundry room, and a door that is stuck.

Stenmark, Victoria. *The Singing Chick.* Henry Holt & Company, 1999. One day, an egg rolls into the forest. It hatches, and out pops a bright yellow chick. The chick is so happy to be alive that he starts singing and doesn't stop, even when a fox swallows him up.

The Wind, the Sun, and the Whistling Traveler

The Wind and the Sun were brother and sister. As you know, brothers and sisters sometimes do not get along. One day they argued about who was stronger.

The Wind said,

"I can blow the trees until they drop their leaves.
I can blow the seas until the waves rise high.
I can blow the rooftop from the castle of a king.
No one, no one is stronger than I!"

The Sun said,

"Until I rise, the day does not begin.
Unless I shine, the seeds do not sprout.
Without my light, no one has sight.
No one is stronger than I, no doubt."

The Wind spotted a traveler, walking down a country road. "Here is the challenge," said the Wind. "The first one to make that traveler remove his coat is the strongest."

"Agreed," said the Sun. "You go first." So the Sun hid behind a cloud, and watched as the Wind began to blow. At first, it was just a breeze. Soon it was gust! As the Wind blew harder and harder, the traveler held his coat tighter and tighter. Finally, the Wind gave up.

The Sun took his turn. At first, he peaked out only a little from behind the cloud. Then he showed his full face. The traveler soon found it too hot to walk with his coat on. He took it off, put it over his shoulder, and went whistling down the road.

Adapted from Aesop's fables.

Tips for telling: *When the wind blows, coach the children to blow gently, then blow as hard as they can. When the sun shines, coach the children to peak out from behind their hands, then hold their hands beside their faces with fingers out like the rays of the sun.*

"MUSIC" Patterns

Rhythm Shaker

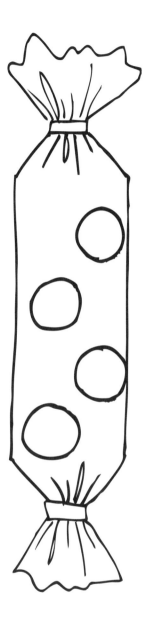

Directions
Collect enough toilet paper tubes or paper towel tubes so you have one for each child. Put a few dried beans or peas inside the tube, and then wrap it with tissue paper or gift wrap. Secure the ends tightly with invisible tape. At storytime, have the children decorate their shaker with stickers. Put on some music and let everyone shake in rhythm.

 This craft takes 10 minutes to complete, including the rhythm activity.

 Rhythm Shaker

My Body

Before Sharing Books

Display some things that one needs to keep the body strong and healthy—fruits, milk, running shoes, soap, a pillow and blanket, etc. Ask the children to tell you how each of these items can make the body healthy. Lead the discussion towards eating well, getting enough rest, getting enough exercise, and playing safely.

Literacy Tip for Parents

Point out shapes throughout the day, including two-dimensional and three-dimensional shapes. "The door is a rectangle. This orange is a sphere. The note pad is a square. The juice can is a cylinder."

Rhymes, Songs, and Fingerplays

Action Rhyme

Upon a Mountain Top
Bodily-Kinesthetic Intelligence

Once upon a mountain top,
A billy goat did stand.
(Touch hands high over head.)
Down he ran, and ran and ran!
(Pat hands on lap quickly.)
Running feels so grand.

Once in a blooming apple tree,
A caterpillar crept.
(Walk fingers up arm).
When he got to the very top,
He curled in a ball and slept.
(Lay face on hands and close eyes.)

Poem

Yummy Food
Naturalist Intelligence

Apples, peaches, cherries, pears,
Yummy food for little bears.
Purple plums and berries blue,
Are good food for children, too.

(You may want to make a flannel board or magnet board set and put up each fruit as you say the poem.)

Action Rhymes

Let's "B" Safe
Bodily-Kinesthetic Intelligence and Letter Recognition

Little b climbed up a tree.
Big B climbed up, too.
They tumbled down and hit the ground,
And they cried and they cried, "Boo hoo."

Little b bounced on the bed.
Big B bounced on it, too.
They bumped their noses,
And stubbed their toeses,
And they cried and they cried,
"Boo hoo."

Little b played with building blocks.
Big B played with them, too.

They played fair and tried to share,

And they laughed and they laughed, "Woo hoo."
Little b ran across the lawn.
Big B ran there, too.
They played fair, and enjoyed the fresh air,
And they laughed and they laughed, "Woo hoo."

Song

"Be Safe"
Tune: "My Bonnie Lies Over the Ocean"

Be safe when you play on the playground.
Be safe when you play with your toys.
Be safe when you play with your best friend.
Be safe, little girls and boys.
Be safe, be safe,
Be safe when you play, be safe, be safe.
Be safe, be safe,
Be safe when you play, be safe!

(Suggestion: Use "Bee Safe" stick puppet while singing.)

Bounce Rhyme for Infant Storytime

Matthew, Mark, Luke, John,
Hold my horse till I leap on.
Hold him steady, hold him sure,
And I'll get over the misty moor.
Blow, wind blow! And go, mill, go!
That the miller may grind his corn.
That the baker may take it,
And into bread make it,
And bring us a loaf in the morn.

Nursery Rhyme for Cultural Awareness

Bobby Shaftoe went to sea,
Silver buckles on his knee.
He'll come back and marry me,
Pretty Bobby Shaftoe.

Books to Share

Carle, Eric. *From Head to Toe.* HarperCollins, 1997. This colorful book introduces basic body parts and movements by encouraging children to imitate the movements of animals. Are you ready? Here we go! Move yourself from head to toe.

Child, Lauren. *I Will Never Not Ever Eat a Tomato.* Candlewick Press, 2000. Charlie convinces his little sister Lola, a picky eater, to try new foods by telling her that carrots are little orange twiglets from Jupiter, mashed potatoes are cloud fluff, and peas are rare green drops from Greenland that fall from the sky.

Livingston, Irene. *Finklehopper Frog.* Ten Speed Press, 2003. Finklehopper Frog puts on his colorful jogging suit to join the other animals, all of which are wearing running shoes and sweat bands and carrying water bottles while they exercise. When some animals laugh at his outfit, one friend encourages Finklehopper to be himself.

Price, Hope Lynne. *These Hands.* Hyperion, 1999. A young girl uses her hands to clap, fly a kite, hold open a book, and create. With rhyming text, this book shows the great potential in every child.

Sweeney, Joan. *Me and My Amazing Body.* Crown Books, 2000. A girl gives a tour of her amazing body, from muscles that stretch and shrink like rubber bands to the heart that works like a little engine. Skin, brain, lungs, stomach, and more are explained and illustrated in a colorful cartoon style.

The Smell of the Bread

In a small town, there was a bakery. Every morning, the baker arrived very early to make bread. He kneaded the dough, shaped the loaves, and set them to rise. When they were very light, he put them in the oven. The smell of the baking bread was wonderful.

Every morning the shop was very busy. Many people in the town came to buy the wonderful thick, brown bread. However, one man came each day and sat in front of the bakery. He never went inside to buy the bread because he was too poor.

One winter morning, after the morning rush was over, the baker saw this poor man sitting outside the bakery. He stormed outside and said to the man, "You are stealing the smell of my bread."

"I have stolen nothing from you, sir," said the poor man.

"I have seen you here many times sitting near my door. You come to smell my bread, but you never pay for it."

"I am not eating your bread," said the poor man. "I do not owe you any money."

"I say you owe me. You have been smelling my bread for free. Let's ask the judge."

So the baker and the poor man walked to the courthouse to speak to the judge. The judge listened carefully to the baker and said, "This is a difficult problem." He thought for a few minutes and then asked the poor man, "Do you have any money?"

"Sir, only a little," he answered. The poor man took a small leather purse from his shirt. He opened it and showed the judge. There were 10 pennies in it. "This is all I have," he said.

"Shake the bag," the judge said to the poor man. The poor man gave the bag a couple of shakes. The coins jingled.

"Listen to that sound," the judge said to the baker. "The sound of the poor man's coins should more than pay for the smell of your bread."

Traditional Jewish folktale.

Bee Safe Stick Puppet

Directions
Copy the stick puppet pattern for each child and cut it out. Have the children color their puppet with markers or crayons. Attach a craft stick using a glue stick or tape. After they have finished the craft, sing the "Be Safe" song once again with everyone.

 This craft takes 10 minutes to complete.

New Baby

Before Sharing Books

Bring a baby doll, wrapped in a blanket. Also bring baby powder, bottles, rattles, and other items babies need. Ask the children to tell you about each of the items and how they are used to care for a new baby.

Literacy Tip for Parents

Toddlers understand more words than they say, so be sure to talk to them all day long about what you are doing together.

Rhymes, Songs, and Fingerplays

Action Rhyme

Surprise
Bodily-Kinesthetic Intelligence

Mommy and Daddy brought home a surprise,
(Hands by face, look surprised.)
A new baby sister with beautiful eyes.
(Pretend to rock baby in arms.)
She sleeps and she wets,
And she coos and she cries.
(Head on hands, draw tears on face.)
She can't say my name yet,
But sometimes she tries. *(Shake head, point to mouth.)*

Song

"My Baby Song"
Tune: "My Bonnie Lies Over the Ocean"
Musical-Rhythmic Intelligence

My baby likes fluffy soft blankets.
My baby likes laughing with glee.
My baby likes shaking her rattle.
My baby likes playing with me.

Baby, baby,
My baby likes playing with me, with me.
Baby, baby,
My baby likes playing with me.

Rhymes

Bounce Rhymes for Infant Storytime

Davy Davy Dumpling,
Boil him in a pot.
Sugar him and butter him,
And eat him while he's hot.

Horsie, horsie, don't you stop,
Just let your feet go clipetty clop.
Your tail goes swish, and the wheels go round,
Giddyup, you're homeward bound.

Nursery Rhyme for Cultural Awareness

Rock-a-bye, baby,
In the tree top.
When the wind blows,
The cradle will rock.
When the bough breaks,
The cradle will fall,
And down will come baby,
Cradle and all.

Books to Share

Blackstone, Stella. ***Baby High, Baby Low.*** Barefoot Books, 1998. Depicts contrasting pairs of babies, including quick and slow, happy and sad, hot and cold.

Cullen, Catherine Ann. ***Thirsty Baby.*** Little, Brown and Company, 2003. Silly story about a baby who drinks his bottle but wants MORE!

Cutler, Jane. ***Darcy and Gran Don't Like Babies.*** Farrar, Straus and Giroux, 2002. Darcy and Gran say they don't like babies, especially Darcy's baby brother, but

after a day in the park doing things baby cannot do they begin to think differently.

Gliori, Debi. ***Mr. Bear's New Baby.*** Scholastic, 1999. Mr. and Mrs. Bear and the other forest animals don't know how to stop Baby Bear from crying, but Small Bear knows just what to do.

Root, Phyllis. ***What Baby Wants.*** Candlewick Press, 1998. Family members try to stop baby from crying, but only his brother figures out what baby wants.

Goldilocks and the Three Bears

Once upon a time, there was a little girl named Goldilocks. She was a very curious little girl. She liked to explore. So one day she went for a walk in the forest. She walked a long, long way, much farther than she had ever walked before. To her surprise, she found a clearing in the forest. And in the clearing, she came upon a little house. She knocked on the door, but no one answered. Being very curious, she went inside anyway.

Goldilocks explored the whole house. First she went to the kitchen. She smelled something delicious! At the table in the kitchen, there were three bowls of porridge. Goldilocks was hungry, so she tasted the porridge from the first bowl.

"This porridge is too hot!" she exclaimed.

Next, she tasted the porridge from the second bowl.

"This porridge is too cold," she said

Finally, she tasted the last bowl of porridge.

"Ahhh, this porridge is just right," she said happily and she ate it all up.

After she'd eaten the three bears' breakfasts she decided she was feeling a little tired. So she walked into the living room where she saw three chairs. Goldilocks sat in the first chair to rest her feet.

"This chair is too hard!" she exclaimed.

So she sat in the second chair.

"This chair is too soft!" she whined.

So she tried the last and smallest chair.

"Ahhh, this chair is just right," she sighed. But just as she settled down into the chair to rest, it broke into pieces! She was very frightened, and she cried just a little. But she was still curious so she decided to explore upstairs. "Maybe there are beds up there," she said.

She went upstairs to the bedroom. She climbed up onto the first bed, but it was too hard. Then she pulled herself into the second bed, but it was too soft. Finally she lay down in the third bed and it was just right. Goldilocks was very comfortable, and soon she fell asleep.

As she was sleeping, the three bears came home. As soon as they walked in the door, they knew someone had been in the house. First they went to the kitchen.

"Someone's been eating my porridge," growled Papa bear.

"Someone's been eating my porridge," said Mama bear.

"Someone's been eating my porridge and they ate it all up!" cried the baby bear.

Next they went to the sitting room. Of course they could tell that someone had been there, too.

"Someone's been sitting in my chair," growled Papa bear.

"Someone's been sitting in my chair," said Mama bear.

"Someone's been sitting in my chair and they've broken it all to pieces," cried the baby bear.

They decided to look around some more. When they got upstairs to the bedroom, Papa bear growled, "Someone's been sleeping in my bed."

"Someone's been sleeping in my bed, too," said Mama bear.

"Someone's been sleeping in my bed and she's still there!" exclaimed Baby bear.

Just then, Goldilocks woke up and saw the three bears. She screamed, "Help!" And she jumped up and ran out of the room. Goldilocks ran down the stairs, opened the door, and ran away into the forest. She ran all the way home. After that, she was not so curious. She never walked into a house when no one was at home. And she never returned to the home of the three bears.

Traditional European folktale.

Baby in a Blanket

Directions
Cut a 12" square of soft flannel fabric for each child. Copy the baby doll pattern and cut it out. Allow the children to color the baby doll, and then wrap it carefully in the flannel blanket.

 This craft takes 5 minutes to complete.

noise

Before Sharing Books

Bring a variety of things that make noise—a phone, a whistle, a baby rattle, and a bell, for example. You may even bring a toy fire truck, and toy animals. With the children, make the noises for each item. Now that they have all their noises out, the children should be ready to sit quietly for stories.

Literacy Tip for Parents

Acquiring the ability to read is a process that begins in infancy. Repeating favorite rhymes and songs often with your child helps him or her learn new vocabulary and get the flow and feel of language.

Rhymes, Songs, and Fingerplays

Song

"The Boys on the Mat"
Tune: "The Wheels on the Bus"

The boys on the mat go,
Pat, pat, pat,
Pat, pat, pat,
Pat pat, pat.
The boys on the mat go,
Pat, pat, pat.
What do you think of that?
(Boys pat hands on lap while singing.)

The girls make a wish and,
Swish, swish, swish,
Swish, swish, swish,
Swish, swish, swish.
The girls make a wish and,
Swish, swish, swish.
What do you think of that?
(Girls brush hands on clothes to make a swishing noise.)

The hands in my lap go,
Clap, clap, clap,
Clap, clap, clap,
Clap, clap, clap.
The hands in my lap go,
Clap, clap, clap.
What do you think of that?
(All children clap hands while singing.)

Rhyme

Big N and Little N
Big N and Little N

Needed a break,
So they went outside for
Some noise to make!
They made a loud noise,
Nearly a yell! *(Shout hey.)*
They made a softer noise,
Nice, like a bell. *(Ring.)*
They made a quiet noise,
Not more than a hush. *(Shh!)*
Big N made a kissing noise, *(Smack!)*
It made Little N blush.
Now Big N and Little N,
Knew it was noon,
So they went in and ate,
Noodle soup with a spoon.

Action Rhymes

Bounce Rhymes for Infant Storytime

One, two, three, four,
Mary's at the cottage door.
Five, six, seven, eight,
Eating cherries off a plate.

Higglety, pigglety, pop!
The dog has ate the mop.
The pig's in a hurry,
The cat's in a flurry,
Higglety, pigglety, pop.

Nursery Rhyme for Cultural Awareness

I'm a little teapot short and stout.
Here is my handle, here is my spout.
When I get all steamed up I will shout,
Tip me over and pour me out.

Books to Share

Feiffer, Jules. **_Bark, George._** HarperCollins, 1999. When George's mother tells her son to bark, he meows. This can't be right, because George is a dog. When George also quacks, oinks, and moos, his mother takes him to the vet to see what is wrong. The vet reaches deep inside the pup and pulls out a cat and more.

Hort, Lenny. **_The Seals on the Bus._** Henry Holt & Company, 2000. The people on the bus are amazed as animals on the bus begin to make many different noises.

O'Connell, Rebecca. **_The Baby Goes Beep._** Roaring Brook Press, 2003. A toddler's busy day includes driving in his car seat, playing with pots, and taking a bath, all with appropriate noises. This book is sure to please the toddlers.

Taylor, Thomas. **_The Loudest Roar._** Scholastic, 2002. A small tiger goes about the jungle roaring at everyone, which makes the jungle anything but peaceful. When the other animals put their heads and their voices together the little tiger is in for a surprise!

Boy Who Cried Wolf

Once, on a hill near a sleepy village, a shepherd boy watched a flock of sheep. Day after day, he tended the sheep. He walked with them, he sat with them, and he even sometimes slept with them. Every day was just the same as the day before. One day, the shepherd boy was desperate for a bit of fun. So he stood at the top of the hill and shouted as loudly as he could,

"Wolf! Wolf! Wolf! Come quick! Come now! The wolf got to my flock somehow!"

Every person in the village heard his cries. The men dropped their tools. The women dropped their pies. They ran up the hill, all out of breath, and looked around. The flock was peacefully grazing. No wolf was anywhere in sight. The boy giggled and pointed to the crowd and said, "I fooled you all! What a funny trick. There is no wolf, but you sure came quick!"

The people shook their heads and went back to their work. They forgave the shepherd boy for the trick. But not many days later, the boy stood at the top of the hill again and shouted, "Wolf! Wolf! Wolf! Come quick! Come now! The wolf got to my flock somehow!"

Just as before, every person in the village heard the boy. They rushed up the hill, huffing and puffing. But soon they could see that the boy was just bluffing. The boy pointed and laughed at them all and said, "I fooled you all! What a funny trick. There is no wolf, but you sure came quick!"

This time, the people were not so forgiving. "Do you think we don't have to work for a living? Do you think all of us have nothing else to do but to run up this hill every time you say boo?" Every man and woman turned and walked away. The shepherd boy was sorry, at least for a day.

For many days after that, the shepherd boy tended his flock well. He walked with the sheep. He sat with the sheep. Sometimes, he slept with the sheep. Every day was the same, until the day that a wolf really did come along. The wolf snarled, and he snatched a sheep in his jaws! The poor sheep cried out in pain! The shepherd boy poked the wolf with his stick, but the wolf did not drop the sheep. The shepherd boy hit the wolf on the head with his stick, but the wolf did not drop the sheep.

The boy knew he needed help. He stood at the top of the hill and shouted, "Wolf! Wolf! Wolf! This time it's real. There's a wolf in my flock. He's having a meal!"

The people in the town heard the boy's cries. No one dropped their tools. No one dropped their pies. No one came along, huffing and puffing. They were sure this time that the boy was bluffing.

The shepherd boy lost all of his sheep that day. In fact, the wolf nearly ate him, too! That's when he learned that no one believes a liar, even when he tells the truth.

Adapted from Aesop's fables.

Little Teapot Color Sheet

I'm A Little Teapot

I'm a little teapot, short and stout.
Here is my handle, here is my spout.
When I get all steamed up I will shout,
Tip me over and pour me out.

Directions
Copy the color sheet for each child. Teach
the rhyme/song to the children, and then
give them crayons or markers for coloring.
Encourage the children to teach someone else
this rhyme, such as Daddy or Grandma.

 **This craft and activity takes
10 minutes to complete.**

Shapes and Sizes

Before Sharing Books

Arrange objects of various shapes and sizes on your table. For example: square blocks, round oranges, rectangle graham crackers, etc. Ask the children to identify the shape as you hold each one up. Ask the children to help you put them in size order.

Literacy Tip for Parents

Include spontaneous math activities in your daily routine. Count the stairs as you climb them, count the bites as your child eats them, or ask your child if there are enough cookies on the plate for everyone at the table.

Rhymes, Songs, and Fingerplays

Action Rhyme

Roundie
Spatial Intelligence
Roundie, roundie,
Bounce so high.
Roundie, roundie,
Fly, fly, fly.
Roundie, roundie,
Roll on the floor
Roundie, roundie,
Roll through the door.

(Make a simple stick puppet to use with this rhyme from the patterns on page 90. You may want to give one to each child to take home to reinforce the rhyme.)

Song

"Draw a Square in the Air"
Tune: "If You're Happy and You Know It"
Musical-Rhythmic Intelligence and Spatial Intelligence

Draw a square in the air, in the air.
Draw a square in the air, in the air.
Draw one here, draw one there,
Draw two, you have a pair.
Draw a square in the air, in the air.

Song

"Heart, Star, Diamond, Square"
Tune: "Head, Shoulders, Knees, and Toes"
Musical-Rhythmic Intelligence and Spatial Intelligence

Heart, star, diamond, square,
Diamond, square.
Shapes, here and everywhere,
Everywhere.
On my clothes and in my hair!
Heart, star, diamond, square,
Diamond, square.

(Cut out the mini shapes from page 90 and tape them to a doll or puppet. As you sing the song, touch the appropriate shape. You may also want to wear clothes with heart, diamond, star, or square shapes on them.)

Rhymes

Bounce Rhymes for Infant Storytime

Father, Mother and Uncle John,
Went to market one by one.
Father fell off—
Mother fell off—
But Uncle John went on and on and on and on and on …

(Bounce the child on your knee while reciting this rhyme. When "Father fell off" and "Mother fell off," dip the child down towards the floor. For "Uncle John went on and on," bounce faster.)

Dance to your daddy,
My little baby,
Dance to your daddy,
My little lamb.
You shall have fishy,
In a little dishy.
You shall have fishy,
When the boat comes in.

(Dance and twirl with child while reciting the rhyme.)

Bouncing baby, bundle of joy.
Mommy's darling, Daddy's boy.

Nursery Rhyme for Cultural Awareness

I see the moon and the moon sees me.
God bless the moon and God bless me.

Books to Share

Baranski, Joan. *Round Is a Pancake.* Penguin, 2001. As this make-believe town prepares a feast for the king, a simple rhyme lists round items.

Dodds, Dayle Ann. *The Shape of Things.* Candlewick Press, 1994. A square becomes a house, a circle becomes a ferris wheel, a triangle is transformed into a sailboat, and a rectangle becomes a train in this colorful concept book. This older title is available, and is an excellent read aloud.

Robert, Francois. *Find A Face.* Chronicle Books, 2004. If you look hard enough, you can find a face in the most unexpected places: on a light switch, a shoe, a cardboard box, or a map. Look around.

Thong, Roseanne. *Round Is a Mooncake: A Book of Shapes.* Chronicle Books, 2000. Through the eyes of a Chinese girl, various shapes are introduced. The rhyming text describes things like dim sum, inking stones, and lucky money.

Three Billy Goats Gruff

Once there were three billy goats. The billy goats were brothers, and their last name was Gruff. After spending a long winter in the valley, the Billy Goats Gruff were ready for a change. They decided to climb to the mountains to eat the new spring grass.

They walked along and walked along until they came to a river that rushed along fast, because it was full of melted snow. They could never wade across it. They would be washed away for sure! The billy goats searched the river until they found a bridge. The billy goats didn't know that a terrible troll lived under the bridge. The troll never, never let anyone cross it. If anyone tried, he ate them up!

The smallest Billy Goat Gruff was the first to reach the bridge. As he crossed, his little hooves went trip trap trip trap trip trap. The troll woke up and growled, "Who is that crossing my bridge?"

"Billy Goat Gruff," said the little billy goat, in his tiny billy goat voice.

"It's time for my breakfast. I'm going to eat you up!" said the troll.

"I'm too small to taste very good," said the little Billy Goat Gruff. "You should wait for my brother to come along."

The troll was really hungry, and he wanted a big breakfast. "All right, you can cross my bridge," he said. "I'll eat you when you come back, and you are nice and fat." So the little billy goat skipped across the bridge and found some delicious grass to eat.

The middle Billy Goat Gruff was the next to reach the bridge. As he crossed, his middle-sized hooves went trip trap trip trap trip trap. The troll's stomach growled with hunger and he shouted, "Who is that crossing my bridge?"

"Billy Goat Gruff," said the middle billy goat, in his middle-sized billy goat voice.

"It's time for my breakfast. I'm going to eat you up!" growled the troll.

"I'm too small to taste very good," said the middle Billy Goat Gruff. "My brother is coming, and he is much bigger."

The troll thought about how delicious the bigger goat would taste and he said, "All right, you can cross my bridge, but hurry and get fat so I can eat you later." The middle billy goat skipped across the bridge and found some delicious grass to eat.

The biggest Billy Goat Gruff came to the bridge. As he crossed, his big hooves went TRIP TRAP TRIP TRAP TRIP TRAP on the wooden bridge. The troll shouted, "Who is that crossing my bridge?"

"BILLY GOAT GRUFF," said the goat in his very big voice.

"It is way past time for my breakfast. I'm going to eat you up!" said the troll.

"I don't think so," said the Billy Goat Gruff. He started to cross the bridge. Just then, the troll climbed up on the bridge. He blinked in the bright sunlight. He raised his hairy arms in the air and shouted, "Where are you, Billy Goat Gruff?"

"Right here," said the Billy Goat Gruff. He lowered his horns. He ran across the bridge. He smashed into the troll. Up, up, up into the air flew the troll. Then he came down with a terrible splash into the river. The rushing water carried him away.

"Now it's time for my breakfast," said Billy Goat Gruff. He skipped across the bridge and soon he was eating delicious grass with his brothers.

Retold from a Norwegian folktale.

Roundie Pattern

Mini Shapes Patterns

Roundie Pattern

90 Let's Read! Storytime Crafts Shapes and Sizes

Shape Puzzle

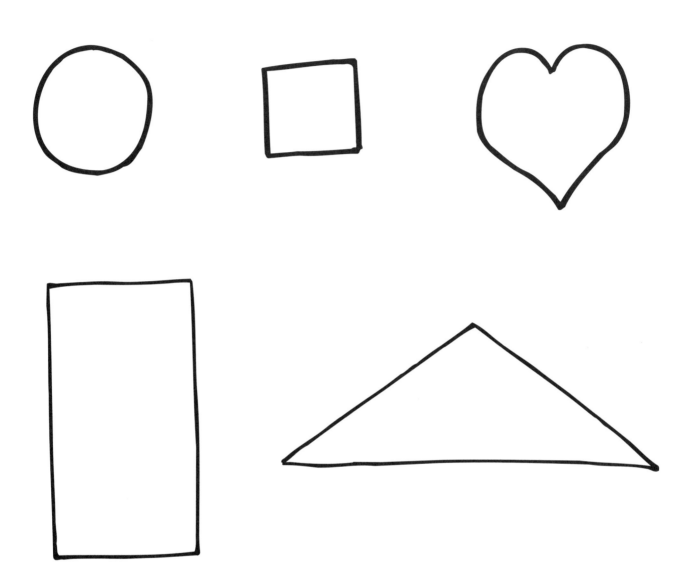

Directions
Copy the patterns for each child and cut them out. Copy the picture from page 92 for each child. At storytime, have the children paste the shape on the matching shape in the illustration. They may also color the picture with crayons or markers.

 This craft takes 10 minutes to complete.

Shape Picture

★ Shape Picture ★

92 Let's Read! Storytime Crafts Shapes and Sizes

Wishes

Before Sharing Books

Discuss with the children traditional ways of making a wish. You may include wishing on a star, blowing out birthday candles to make a wish, wishing on a fallen eyelash, finding a four leaf clover, catching a leprechaun, and tossing a coin in a fountain. Wave your magic wand and ask everyone to wish for good stories.

Literacy Tip for Parents

Research has found that children who are familiar with nursery rhymes when they enter kindergarten often have an easier time learning to read.

Rhymes, Songs, and Fingerplays

Rhyme

Big J and Little J
Letter Recognition

Big J and Little J,
Went out after dark,
For a little jog,
In the park.

The sky turned purple,
Then gray then black.
Little J said,
"We should make our journey back."

Big J saw a star,
Like a jewel in the night.
"Look," he said,
"Star light, Star bright!"

"Make a wish," said Big J.
That's just what Little J did!
Then they jogged back home,
And jumped into bed.

Song

"Make A Wish"
Tune: "Mary Had a Little Lamb"
Musical-Rhythmic Intelligence

Find a clover, make a wish,
Make a wish, make a wish.
Find a clover, make a wish,
I hope your wish comes true.

Repeat with: Blow the candles, Toss a coin, etc. You may use the patterns on page 96 to create magnet board illustrations to use with this song.

Rhymes

Bounce Rhymes for Infant Storytime

The man in the moon,
Came down too soon,
And asked his way to Norwich.
He went by the south,
And burnt his mouth,
While supping cold plum porridge.

The big ship sails on the alley alley oh.
On the alley alley oh.
On the alley alley oh.
The big ship sails on the alley alley oh,
On the last day of September.

Nursery Rhyme for Cultural Awareness

Star light, star bright,
First star I see tonight.
I wish I may, I wish I might,
Have the wish I wish tonight.

Books to Share

Addy, Sharon Hart. *When Wishes Were Horses.* Houghton Mifflin, 2002. A boy is carrying a heavy sack of flour home from the store in the town of Dusty Gulch. He sees a stranger on horseback and wishes he had a horse. With a wink from the stranger, the wish is granted. Each time he says the words "I wish" another horse of a different color appears. Soon he is surrounded by a herd of them, and the folks in town are getting confused!

Bridges, Shirin Yim. *Ruby's Wish.* Chronicle Books, 2002. Ruby lives in a large Chinese family at the turn of the twentieth century. She is not like the other girls. She always wears red, and she is the only girl in the large family who continues to study while also doing all of the household work assigned to her. Ruby's grandfather discovers that Ruby has a secret wish, and he wisely watches over her, waiting for the right time to surprise her.

Dunbar, Joyce. *The Pig Who Wished.* DK Publishing, 2000. A pig swallows a magic acorn, and suddenly all her wishes come true. She eats cream puffs in a tea shop, and goes home with a toddler who loves having a pig riding in his stroller. Everything is great for the pig, until a hiccup brings the acorn out and the magic ends. Or does it?

Kirk, Daniel. *Jack and Jill.* Penguin, 2003. Jack and Jill go up the hill to get water for their fish tank, and meet a magical crocodile who lives in the well. He agrees to let the children fill their pail with water if they bring him a meal. This fractured version of the song includes plenty of twists, wishes, and a rescue.

Wolfe, Frances. *One Wish.* Tundra, 2004. A girl wishes for a cottage by the sea. She describes a yellow cottage, surrounded by roses and Queen Anne's lace. The picture-perfect wish includes walking on the beach to find treasures, sailing a boat, and feeding sea gulls.

The Silver on the Hearth

There once was a poor man, who was very hard-working and very honest. Although he worked very hard every day, he could never manage to save even one coin. He decided that if he was ever to have any riches, they would have to simply appear before him. So he wished very hard that one morning he would wake up and discover many coins on his own fireplace hearth. If they were on his own hearth, he would have no doubt that they were meant to be his.

Every morning the man woke up, looked for coins on his hearth, and then went to work. While working one day, he snagged his pants on a thorny bush. So that this would never happen again, he dug around the roots and pulled the bush out of the ground. There in the ground, the man found a clay jar. He dug a little more so he could remove the lid of the jar. He was amazed when he discovered that the jar was filled with silver coins. Of course, he would never keep the coins! This is what he said,

"I wished for treasure on my hearth.

Coins meant for only me.

Someone else may have wished for this.

So I will let it be."

So, the man covered the clay jar again, and left it just where he found it. When he told his wife about it that night while they shared a humble meal of soup and bread, she was very angry with him. "Treasure is treasure," she said. "What does it matter to us if it appears in a clay jar or on our fireplace hearth?" But the man simply would not go and dig it up.

The next day the woman went to her neighbor and told him all about the jar of coins her husband found. "He refuses to dig the treasure up," she said. "Go and get it for yourself, but don't forget I was the one who told you about it!"

The neighbor was very pleased to hear about a jar filled with coins so near! He found the place where the earth had been recently disturbed, near some thorny bushes. He dug the earth and found the clay jar. When he lifted the lid he saw … not treasure. Oh, no! The jar was filled with poisonous snakes. He quickly put the lid back on the pot. He picked it up and carried it back home with him. "Remember who told you about it!" he muttered. "Of course, I remember who told me about it. Just wait until she sees this."

The man waited until darkness fell. Silently he climbed up onto the roof of the woman's house. He opened the clay pot and poured the contents down the chimney. "Treasure, she said. Go dig up the treasure. She wanted the snakes to bite me! I hope they bite her instead."

At the first light of day, the poor and honest man got up. Just as he did every day, he went to his fireplace hearth to see if his wish had come true. What he saw made his eyes open wide! The hearth was covered with silver coins! He scooped them up in his hands, and said,

"I wished for treasure on my hearth,

Coins meant for only me.

I accept this gift today,

And grateful I will be."

Traditional Asian folktale.

Variations of this story are found throughout Asia. One variation is "Fortune and the Woodcutter" from The Brown Fairy Book, edited by Andrew Lang.

"Make a Wish" Patterns

Magic Wand

Directions
Copy the star pattern for each child and cut it out. Have the children color their star. You may choose to allow them to use glitter colored glue (available at craft stores) to add details. Attach the star to a drinking straw with tape.

 This craft takes 10 minutes to complete.

Library Skills Rhymes & Songs

Action Story

This Is the Book
(Use a book as a visual aid while telling this story.)

This is the book I borrowed from the library.

This is the cover of the book I borrowed from the library.

This is the title on the cover of the book I borrowed from the library.

This is the author's name, on the cover of the book I borrowed from the library.

These are the pages in the book I borrowed from the library.

These are the words, on the pages, in the book I borrowed from the library.

These are the pictures, on the pages, in the book I borrowed from the library.

These are the poems, songs, stories, and ideas in the book I borrowed from the library.

This is the smile on my face, because I enjoyed the book I borrowed from the library.

Song

"I Borrowed a Book"
(Sung to the tune: "The Wheels on the Bus")

I borrowed a book from the library,
Library, library.
I borrowed a book from the library,
Just for me.

Additional Verses:
I opened the book from the library.
I turned the pages carefully.
I closed the book from the library.
I returned the book to the library.
I chose another book from the library.

Handouts for Parents

Multiple Intelligences and Your Preschool Child

Howard Gardner's Multiple Intelligences

Linguistic Intelligence: The ability to read, write, and communicate with words.

Logical-Mathematical Intelligence: The ability to reason and calculate.

Musical Intelligence: The musical ability highly developed by composers and top musicians.

Spatial Intelligence: The ability to master position in space. Architects, painters, and pilots use this intelligence.

Visual Intelligence: The ability to memorize visually, and use the imagination.

Bodily-Kinesthetic Intelligence: The physical intelligence used by dancers and athletes.

Social-Interpersonal Intelligence: The ability to relate to others, used by salespeople and motivators.

Intrapersonal (Self Awareness) Intelligence: The ability to know one's inner feelings, wants, and needs.

Naturalist Intelligence: The ability to learn by exploring nature.

You can increase your child's ability to learn by providing him or her with an enriched environment. Provide play activities that stimulate each of the types of intelligences. Since your child is constantly learning, there will be many chances each day for you to engage in spontaneous learning activities. Your child learns best when:

- He or she feels connected to the adults in his or her life.
- He or she is interested and actively engaged.
- He or she is enjoying the activity.

Here are some activities you can do with your child to strengthen each of the intelligences:

- Make up stories together, the sillier the better.
- Ask your child questions as you go about your day, such as "Did you hear the fire engine?"
- Allow your child to help you measure ingredients for recipes.
- Compare sizes and shapes. "Whose shoes are bigger, mine or yours?"
- Ask your child to find the first letter of his or her name on the packages at the grocery store.
- Sing a few notes, and ask your child to echo you. This teaches pitch and rhythm.
- Build bridges and roads for toy cars using household items (shoeboxes, dishes, etc.).
- Make up a little play, using puppets or dolls for the characters.
- Provide drawing paper and crayons for your child. Use coloring books together.
- Turn on some music and dance together.
- Count the stop signs from your home to the store.
- Play catch using a variety of objects of different sizes and weights.
- Go to the playground to strengthen balance and climbing skills.
- Teach your child a polite phrase or greeting (good morning, how are you, pleased to meet you, etc.). See how many times you can repeat it during the day.
- Spontaneously ask, "How do you feel right now?" Teach appropriate responses such as, "I feel hungry," "I feel happy," "I feel curious," "I feel excited," "I feel tired," "I feel hot."
- Start a collection together of natural objects, such as leaves, butterflies, rocks, shells, and seeds. Learn to identify them together.
- Using illustrated books, learn to identify as many dinosaurs as you can.
- Listen to the bird songs while going for a walk. Try to imitate the sounds. Can you name the bird that makes each sound?

Fitting Read Aloud Time into Your Day

What do children learn from being read to?

- Reading is fun
- Pictures give clues to the story
- The print goes from left to right
- Print represents words
- Stories have a beginning, a middle, and an end
- New vocabulary is learned in context

When can you find reading time?

- After lunch to prepare for rest time
- While waiting for doctor or dentist
- While dinner is in the oven
- While the child is in the bathtub
- Bedtime

What should you read?

- Books you like
- Books with fun, repetitive phrases
- Books with a clear beginning, middle, and end
- Books with lots of action
- Easy nonfiction on a subject your child likes
- Magazines, comics from the newspaper, recipes, letters, e-mail

How can you make the most of reading aloud?

- Preview the book so you are familiar with it before reading aloud
- Read with expression—be excited, pause for a moment, whisper, laugh
- Use your voice creatively to make funny sounds or characters
- Read slowly
- Let your child turn the pages, or say repetitive phrases with you
- Repeat the book if the child really enjoys it

Simple Storytelling Techniques for Families

Try any of the following ideas to include storytelling as part of the fun you and your child share. Telling stories together will increase your child's vocabulary, prepare him or her for reading, and enhance his or her social skills. Sharing this activity with your child will be fun for both of you!

- Use three sizes of spoons as the "characters" as you retell a familiar folktale such as "Goldilocks and the Three Bears," "The Three Little Pigs," or "The Three Billy Goats Gruff."

- Make up your own "how and why" story to explain the unexplainable in your home. Where do missing socks go? Who came through the door when it opened all by itself? Why is there a crack in the wall?

- Create a serial adventure about "when Daddy (or Mommy) was little" and add to it every day.

- Create your own superhero and make up stories about how he or she could rescue your family.

- Make up a story about the food on your child's plate as he or she eats dinner. "Mandy's peas went on an adventure. They climbed a mashed potato mountain. They sloshed through the applesauce river, and then they jumped over the bread fence right into Mandy's mouth!"

- Put a sock on your hand to create an instant puppet. Give him or her something silly to say!

- Make up a story about the adventures your child's shoes have at night while he or she is sleeping. Do they go swimming in the ocean? Do they fly in a rocket to another planet? Do they follow the rainbow to a magical place?

- Tell your child a true story about how your family came to own a certain possession, such as your pet, your piano, or a flower vase.

- Tell stories about a family member who is traveling or who lives in another town. "Grandma had a visitor in her garden today. It was a bunny with a pink nose. He hopped over to Grandma, wiggled his nose and …"

- During a rainstorm, make up a story about the thirsty little flowers who love the rain.

- At bath time, make up an adventure about the bar of soap floating across the sea to a tropical island.

Recipes for Parents and Children to Make Together

No Bake Peanut Butter Balls

- ½ cup peanut butter
- ½ cup honey
- 2 tablespoons powdered milk
- 1 cup crushed cornflakes cereal

Set the cornflakes aside. Mix all of the other ingredients well. Roll the dough into balls. Then roll the balls in cornflakes until covered.

Frozen Bananas

- 1 banana
- 2 Popsicle sticks
- Optional: honey, peanut butter, Rice Krispies® cereal, or coconut

Peel a firm, ripe banana and cut it in half. Insert a Popsicle stick in each half. Wrap in plastic and freeze. When the banana is frozen and ready to eat, dip it in peanut butter, honey, cereal, or coconut.

Orange Frosts

- 2 cups milk
- 1 cup water
- 1 cup ice cubes
- 3 T sugar
- 6 oz can frozen orange juice concentrate

Combine all of the ingredients in a blender. Puree until smooth and the ice cubes are chopped.

Potato Pancakes

- 2 cups mashed potatoes
- 2 tablespoons flour
- 1 egg
- margarine
- applesauce *(optional)*

Mix the first three ingredients. Make them into patties. Fry in margarine a few minutes on each side, until golden brown. Serve with applesauce if you like.

Turkey Wrap

- 1 flour tortilla, white or flavored
- 1 tablespoon mayonnaise
- 3 slices thinly sliced turkey
- 3 slices thinly sliced cheese
- 2 tablespoons shredded carrot

Spread the mayonnaise on the tortilla. Arrange turkey and cheese slices on mayonnaise. Top with shredded carrot. Roll up and serve.

Ants on a Log

- celery sticks
- peanut butter
- raisins

Wash the celery sticks and cut them into 4-inch lengths. Dry them with a paper towel. Spread peanut butter in the celery sticks and top with raisins.

Baked Apples with Raisins and Nuts

- 4 apples
- ½ cup chopped walnuts
- ½ cup raisins
- ½ cup apple juice
- ½ cup water
- 2 tablespoons honey
- 2 tablespoons butter

Peel and core the apples. Place the apples in a greased 8-inch baking pan. Fill the apples with walnuts and raisins. Pour the apple juice and water over the apples, then pour honey on the apples. Dot each apple with butter. Cover the pan with foil and bake 40 minutes at 350 degrees. Remove the apples from the oven and baste with juice from the pan. Serve warm. You may serve with ice cream if desired.

Muffins

- 1¾ cup flour
- ¼ cup sugar
- 1 egg
- 1 teaspoon salt
- 2 tablespoons baking powder
- ¾ cup milk
- ⅓ cup vegetable oil
- 1 teaspoon vanilla

Mix the dry ingredients. Add the egg, milk, vanilla, and oil. Stir until just moistened. You may add any of the following: 1 cup fresh blueberries, 1 cup shredded carrots, or 1 cup mashed banana. Spoon into greased or paper-lined muffin tins. Bake at 400° for 15 minutes or until golden brown on top. Makes 12.

Home Art Activities for Parent and Child

Paper Plate Portrait

Supplies:
- white paper plate
- crayons or markers
- glue *(optional)*
- macaroni, cut yarn, colored paper *(optional)*

Use crayons or markers to draw a self portrait on a paper plate. For a three dimensional portrait, glue on macaroni, cut yarn, or colored paper.

Gift Bags

Supplies:
- brown paper bags or used gift bags
- old greeting cards
- scissors
- glue

Cut out pictures from old greeting cards. Glue them on to brown paper bags or used gift bags to make new, unique gift bags.

Sweet Smelling Water Color Pictures

Supplies:
- 8 oz paper cups
- several packages flavored drink mix
- water
- paintbrush
- newsprint or other plain paper

Pour one package of drink mix into a paper cup. Mix with 2 tablespoons warm water and stir until well dissolved. Repeat with each color. Use these paints to paint on the newsprint for a sweet-smelling picture.

Easy Play Dough

Supplies:
- 1 cup flour
- 4 tablespoons salt
- 2 tablespoons warm water
- food coloring

In a mixing bowl, stir flour and salt together. Add the water slowly, stirring until well moistened. Add a few drops of food coloring and knead the dough until the color is well mixed. Use the dough to create a variety of shapes with hands, or roll out and cut with cookie cutters. Keep the dough covered in the refrigerator for future use, or let your creations air dry.

Thumbprint Art

Supplies:
- ink pad
- drawing paper
- felt-tip pens

Make a thumb print by pressing your thumb on the ink pad and then applying it to the drawing paper. Using the felt-tip pen, add features to create animals, faces, flowers, bugs, or whatever you can imagine. You may use this technique to create unique gift cards as well.

Cotton Swab Painting

Supplies:
- cotton swabs
- tempera paint
- newsprint or other plain paper
- pie tin

Place about one teaspoon of several colors of tempera paint in a pie tin. This will be the palate. Use cotton swabs for paintbrushes. Dip the cotton swab in the paint, and then draw with it on the newsprint.

Checklist for Storytellers

These elements should be regularly included in storytimes, but it is not necessary to include each one at every storytime.

Book Skills

- ❏ Show cover
- ❏ Tell title and author
- ❏ Turn pages carefully

Listening Skills

- ❏ How to sit comfortably
- ❏ Save comments and questions to the end
- ❏ Ask questions about the book after reading

Library Skills

- ❏ Borrow and return concept
- ❏ Ask for what you want

Oral Tradition

- ❏ Nursery rhyme
- ❏ Folktale

Story Awareness

- ❏ Retelling skills
- ❏ Character identification

Internalization

- ❏ Identify with protagonist
- ❏ Similarities of habits

Motor Skills

- ❏ Action rhymes or songs
- ❏ Fingerplays
- ❏ Crafts

Music Skills

- ❏ Pitch and rhythm

Natural World

- ❏ Seasons, day and night
- ❏ Identify flowers, animals, dinosaurs
- ❏ Which animals like cold weather

Humor

- ❏ Language skills—word meaning
- ❏ Social skills—appropriate humor

Counting

- ❏ Counting by ones to ten or twenty
- ❏ Counting by tens

Letter Recognition

- ❏ Upper- and lowercase
- ❏ Identify the phonetic sounds of letters

Rhyme

- ❏ Stories with rhyme, nursery rhymes
- ❏ Inventing rhyme spontaneously

Repetition

- ❏ Help children repeat phrase in story
- ❏ Repeat rhymes and songs to aid memory

Connection—child to storyteller

- ❏ Names—use first names when possible
- ❏ Share personal preferences with children
- ❏ Bring personal objects to show
- ❏ Tell them about next storytime to build trust

Statistics

- ❏ Count the number in attendance
- ❏ Make notes about what you used, the date, where you presented this storytime

CT 2006